The Murrays of Murray Hill

Lindley Murray

The *Murrays*
of Murray
Hill

Charles Monaghan

Urban History Press
Brooklyn, New York

For Jenny,
with all my love

Urban History Press
534 Third Street, Brooklyn, New York 11215

Copyright © 1998 Charles Monaghan

Jacket Illustration of Lindley Murray courtesy of The Quaker Collection, Haverford College Library, Haverford, PA 19041

Frontispiece Illustration and signature of Lindley Murray courtesy of the Charles Roberts Autograph Collection, Haverford College Library

Book Design and Production Ed Haggerty Associates Inc., Brooklyn, New York 11215

Library of Congress Cataloging in Publication Data
Monaghan, Charles, 1932–
   The Murrays of Murray Hill
   Bibliography: p.
   Includes index.
     1. Murray, Lindley (1745–1826)   2. Textbooks—United States—
history   3. New York State—history—Revolution 1775–1783
4. Society of Friends—history   5. Enlightenment—Scotland
I. Title
Library of Congress Catalog Card Number 97-62542
ISBN 0-9662430-0-5

Printed in the United States of America.
10 9 8 7 6 5 4 3 2 1
First Edition

Contents

Acknowledgements

THIS BOOK, MODEST IN SCOPE, IS INTENDED to rescue from historical obscurity a merchant family that played an important role in New York City in the late eighteenth and early nineteenth centuries. The story provides a window on how one New York family strove to keep its fortunes afloat at a time—the years immediately before the Revolution, and the war's aftermath—that was glorious to many, disastrous to others.

In particular, the book is aimed at restoring to history the name and accomplishments of the family's eldest child, Lindley Murray, the largest-selling author in the world during the first four decades of the nineteenth century. Exiled as a loyalist, Lindley gained fame throughout the English-speaking world and beyond as a writer of literacy textbooks for schoolchildren.

There are many aspects of the story, often involving considerable research in archives and contemporary newspapers, that should be of interest to historians. These include the accounts of the Murrays' varied business enterprises, Lindley Murray's Enlightenment-style education, the *Beulah* affair of 1775 (in which the Murray family tried to break the nonimportation agreement ordered by the Continental Congress), the calculation of the astounding number of Murray books sold, and the examination of the content of Murray's *English Reader*.

In particular, the analysis of the *English Reader* will, I hope, spur work in two areas only suggested here. One is its likely effect on the spread of anti-slavery sentiments based on Enlightenment civic humanist ideas; many reading texts of the day contained anti-slavery material, but the *English Reader's* enormous circulation made it a special case. Second is the possible effect of Murray's book on the continuity of civic humanist ideas from colonial times into antebellum America. Through the *English Reader,* children in the nation's schools were offered a diet of Enlightenment, civic humanist and republican propositions that dated from a century and more before. In the decades following the American Revolution, political practice may have changed, but a reservoir of older civic humanist and republican sentiments persisted in books such as the *English Reader.*

FOR HIS INTELLIGENCE AND UNFAILING good humor in the design and production of this book, I would like to thank Ed Haggerty of Ed Haggerty Associates Inc., Brooklyn.

Research for *The Murrays of Murray Hill* took place on and off over nearly a decade at numerous libraries in the United States and Britain, and I can mention only a few of the many persons who have helped me.

Elizabeth H. Moger, retired as keeper of the records at the Haviland Room of the Archives of the New York Religious Society of Friends (now housed at Swarthmore College), was wonderfully kind in making available to me the letters of Lindley Murray to his brother John and others, as well as the records of the New York Meeting for Sufferings in the years leading up to the Revolution. She also patiently explained to an outsider various points of Quaker governance.

Emma J. Lapansky and Elisabeth Potts Brown and their staff at the Haverford College Library helped me to explore in their extensive Quaker Collection the connection of the Murrays to the Philadelphia Friends. Mary Ellen Chijioke, Librarian of Swarthmore College, very kindly provided me with xeroxes of Lindley Murray letters from the Friends' Historical Library at Swarthmore.

At the library of the Morristown (N.J.) National Historic Park, Johnnie Rowe, museum technician and registrar, was very helpful with the correspondence of Joseph Hoff, the Murrays' mine manager.

Jean Ashton and her staff at the Columbia University Library were extremely cooperative in allowing me to consult the papers of John Jay as well as Lindley Murray material.

I cannot praise highly enough Nancy Burkett and her knowledgeable and helpful library staff at the American Antiquarian Society in Worcester, Massachusetts; it is a glorious place to do research.

I would also like to thank the library staffs of the New York Public Library, the New-York Historical Society, the Library of Congress, Harvard University, Brown University, the Massachusetts Historical Society, the Brooklyn Public Library, Dalhousie University, the University of Edinburgh, the Scottish Records Office (Edinburgh), the University of St. Andrews, the Bodleian Library of Oxford University, the Rockefeller Library of Cambridge University, and the Library of Friends' House, London.

Many individuals offered help, encouragement and valuable criticism. I am immensely grateful to Ingrid Tieken-Boon van Ostade of the University of Leiden for her meticulous editing of *Two Hundred Years of Lindley Murray* and to all my fellow contributors to that volume, from whom I learned a great deal. The excellence of that volume, and the commentaries of the outstanding grammarians who contributed to it, have lightened my burden of discussing Lindley Murray's grammatical contributions. Others who must be named are James Green of the Library Company of Philadelphia, Cornelia King of the Free Library of Pennsylvania, the inimitable Chris Stray of Swansea University (whose gift of a copy of Lindley Murray's *Memoirs* saved me dozens of hours of library visits), Stephen Spackman of the University of St. Andrews, William Joyce of the Princeton University Library, Charles Cherry of Villanova University,

William Gilmore of Rowan University, James Broussard of Lebanon Valley College, Lynda Mugglestone of Pembroke College, Oxford, Ian Jackson (the antiquarian and bibliophile of Berkeley, California), Ian Michael (the authority on early British literacy textbooks), and the Quaker historians Hugh Barbour and Alson D. Van Wagner. I have also benefited from conversations with and the work of Michael V. Belok, Rosalind Remer, Frances Austin, Linda Conron, David Rawson and David Mikosz.

My dear friend Marvin Gelfand shared with me his immense knowledge of New York City history. My older daughter, Leila Monaghan, encouraged me at every step, offering the valuable viewpoint of a linguistic anthropologist and reading the final manuscript. I also appreciate the encouragement throughout the project of my friends Byron Dobell and Richard Karp. I only wish that Walter Karp, from whom I learned so much, was alive to read the book.

Every morning, I am privileged to wake up next to the leading expert on early American literacy textbooks. My wife, Jennifer Monaghan, has been a scholarly model, invaluable resource, discerning critic and ever-supportive friend.

The Murrays of Murray Hill

The Murrays of Murray Hill—A Genealogy

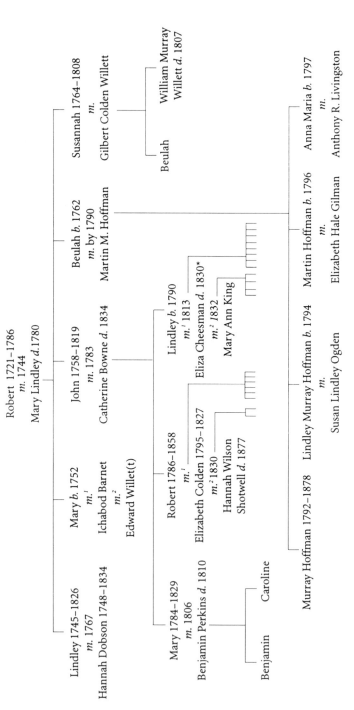

*daughter of Forman Cheesman. See *Dictionary of American Biography.*

On the Trail of the Murrays

1

MANHATTAN ISLAND SITS on an ancient sunken mountain ridge. Atop a billion-year-old layer of gneiss and a somewhat younger, undulating strand of dolomite is a layer of rock geologists call Manhattan schist. In the north, it is close to the surface, but from Columbia University southward, it heads downhill, rising again south of Chambers Street.

For the most part, the dip between Columbia and Chambers Street is filled with detritus left by a glacier of the last Ice Age. On the eastern side of this area, rising gently from Kips Bay, is the neighborhood today known as Murray Hill, which takes its name from the New York merchant family that occupied a farming estate and great house there from about 1762. The estate was known by the German name Inclenberg, or sometimes by the French equivalent, Belmont. Creator of the estate was the paterfamilias of the New York Murrays, Robert Murray (1721–1786). The Murray Hill farm was leased by Robert from the municipality; the land was bought outright by his descendants only in 1799. The plot contained exactly 29 acres, 3 rods and 30 perches of land.

The original Murray Hill farm began a few feet south of today's Thirty-Third Street and extended north to the middle of the block between Thirty-Eighth and Thirty-Ninth Streets. At its southern end, the plot was rather narrow, but at the north it went from about today's Lexington Avenue to a point between

Madison and Fifth Avenues. The Murray mansion, at what is now Park Avenue and Thirty-Seventh Street, was a few hundred yards down a long driveway from the eastern side of the plot. Perched on a since-flattened hill, the house had a view eastwards to Kips Bay and the East River.[1]

This book tells two interconnected stories. One involves the Murray family itself, whose American roots—before the family's arrival in New York in 1753—go back to the Pennsylvania of the early eighteenth century. In New York, the Murrays became connected by marriage with many of the leading personalities of the city in the late eighteenth century. The other story in this book concerns the Murray family's most illustrious member, the eldest son, Lindley Murray, a lawyer who was forced into exile as a loyalist after the Revolution and went on to become an author of international renown.

Robert Murray, Lindley's father, rose from an immigrant miller in the second half of the eighteenth century to become one of New York's leading merchants. The tale of this Quaker family is at its most fascinating and poignant as it faces the vicissitudes and aftermath of the American Revolution. In an enduring New York legend (celebrated in two Broadway plays), the mother, Mary Lindley Murray, and her beautiful daughters, using all their charms, delayed British officers on the day that their army invaded Manhattan, enabling George Washington's troops to escape and fight another day.

Lindley Murray was the largest-selling author in the world in the first four decades of the nineteenth century. His first great success was his *Grammar*, which earned him in the nineteenth century the sobriquet "the Quaker Grammarian." More important, though, was another of his books, his *English Reader*, an anthology that sold an astounding five million copies in the United States before the Civil War. Through its selections, the book helped create an intellectual climate that led to wide acceptance in the North of anti-slavery ideas. Abraham Lincoln, no less, called the *English Reader* "the best schoolbook ever put in the hands of an American youth."

But by the opening of the twentieth century, Lindley, once dubbed by a contemporary "the immortal Murray,"[2] had all but disappeared into the mists of history. Today, just over two centuries since his *Grammar* first appeared, there is a renewal of interest in Lindley Murray. In 1996, a volume of scholarly essays on him and his grammatical work appeared in Germany. In the same year, Routledge/Thoemmes Press in Britain reproduced Murray's educational works, edited by David A. Reibel.[3] The present book, however, is the first extended biographical discussion of the Murray family.

I came to write about Lindley Murray and the Murrays of Murray Hill through the scholarly work of my wife, E. Jennifer Monaghan. She is the author of *A Common Heritage: Noah Webster's Blue-Back Speller* and a leading expert on literacy education in early America.[4] In conjunction with her work, we began several decades ago to collect old literacy textbooks—spellers, primers, readers, grammars and handwriting manuals. Our search entailed many pleasurable visits to old book barns in New England, upstate New York and Pennsylvania. Textbooks were then little valued, and we often found stacks of them moldering in a corner. In addition, as I traveled around the country on writing assignments, I made it a point to find antiquarian bookstores and search out old school texts. Today, our collection amounts to some 1,600 books.

Very early in our search, we noticed how many copies of textbooks we were finding by Lindley Murray. (He had written eleven of them.) My wife was aware of Murray's works from her research on Webster—Murray's grammar had been a serious rival to Webster's and displaced it in public favor in the early years of the nineteenth century. Above all, we found Murray's *English Reader* in astounding abundance. There was hardly a book barn or antiquarian bookstore that we visited in the 1970s and 1980s that did not have one copy or more of the *English Reader* on its shelves or in a dusty corner.

The ubiquity of his textbooks made me wonder about Lindley Murray himself. So I began to do some research. I was shocked at how little information was available, though I did discover his link to the family that gave its name to Murray Hill. Later in my research, I came to focus more attentively on that intriguing clan.

In this book, I look first at the Scotch–Irish and Quaker roots of the Murray family in Pennsylvania. Then I examine Robert Murray's rise as a merchant in the boom times of New York City in the 1750s and 1760s, and the establishment of his famous estate, Inclenberg. The next chapter, which discusses Lindley Murray's education, provides a window on the influence of the European Enlightenment on the American merchant class of the day. In what may be the book's most significant section for students of the history of the American Revolution, I devote two chapters to the Murray family's role in that great event, including the first close examination of the *Beulah* affair, the Murray family's attempt to undermine the nonimportation agreement among the colonies in 1775. After an examination of how pressure by patriots forced Lindley's departure for Britain, I discuss how he took up his pen as a writer of textbooks. I particularly examine his most important work, the *English Reader*. In a final chapter, I trace the fate of Lindley and the Murray family in the succeeding generation. An appendix gives details on the number of Lindley Murray's textbooks published in the United States and Britain. I hope these totals will lead to scholarly reconsideration of his importance.

As I proceeded with work on this book, I was struck more and more by the humanity of it all—how the Murray family struggled to obtain its economic and social position, and then became a victim of the commitments it made to obtain that position. It is a story that shows what it means to have a revolution, how it forces people to choose sides, and how the losers in the battle are punished. It tells, too, what happened in the wake of this upending of society—how people recovered and life went on. An ironic lesson is that if Lindley Murray had simply continued as a prosperous New York lawyer, he would never have written the textbooks that subsequently gained him enduring, if flickering, fame. Yet in his lifetime, Lindley would surely have traded all his renown to leave the precincts of York, England, his place of exile, and once again walk the streets of New York with his beloved wife, Hannah.

2

THE MOST IMPORTANT SOURCE on the Murrays of Murray Hill is Lindley's *Memoirs*. But it is a book that poses a challenging problem. Nearly all of the few previous writers about Lindley Murray have accepted the *Memoirs* at face value. In particular, misled by Murray's avoidance of the subject, they seem not to have realized that Murray was forced into exile from America as a loyalist. The first book on Murray of any sort, Stephen Allott's 86-page *Lindley Murray 1745–1826: Quaker Grammarian of New York and Old York* (1991), a shortened and annotated version of the *Memoirs*, does not question Lindley's cover-up.[5]

The historian, however, must attempt to understand the context in which a document such as the *Memoirs* was produced, and to weigh its assertions against other known facts. When Lindley Murray's *Memoirs* are subjected to such a test, they emerge as a valuable repository of information about Lindley and his family, but they are also deeply flawed, for Lindley systematically attempted to exculpate his conduct before and during the American Revolution. By and large, his attempt succeeded.

Lindley Murray's *Memoirs* were not published until 1826, just after his death. Their form is somewhat unusual. They are composed of six autobiographical letters, begun in the summer of 1806. "They were finished in the spring of 1809," says his secretary, Elizabeth Frank, "and committed to my care in the autumn of that year." Frank added a preface and an afterword that covers the years after 1809. Lindley revised his portion in 1823, three years before his death. In her preface, Elizabeth Frank says that Lindley's autobiographical letters were written in response to a suggestion by her, and in the text Lindley acknowledges that request.[6] While Frank undoubtedly did urge Lindley to set down his autobiographical reminiscences, it is unlikely, as we shall see, that they were composed primarily to be read by her or any residents of Britain. It was a book aimed at protecting Lindley's reputation—and his family's—in the United States.

Whatever the genesis of the *Memoirs*, it is evident that Lindley had no intention of telling the full story of his participation in the events that led up to the Revolution and of his wartime activities. Indeed, he barely mentions the Revolution at all—the event that had shaken the western world and caused his exile—referring to it only in passing as "the troubles in America."[7]

The *Memoirs* are best understood as a brief by an accomplished lawyer (which Lindley was), gathering the facts that make his case stronger, and ignoring facts and actions that would tend to undermine his case. In drawing a veil over his Revolutionary-era activities, Lindley reveals that in his own mind at least, he had something to hide. Yet the *Memoirs* remain an extremely valuable source, fact-filled, and in their way touching, a plea by Lindley for the reader to understand his motives. Lindley's purpose—disguising his wartime activities—was remarkably successful. These activities were never discussed, for example, by his textbook rivals, who certainly would have liked to have had such information at hand.

Over the years, however, several historians have seen through Lindley Murray's story in the *Memoirs*. Lorenzo Sabine, in his compendium of short biographies of loyalists originally published in 1864, includes both Lindley Murray and his father Robert. Years earlier, Sabine had interviewed people who had lived through the Revolution, and his list is considered definitive.[8]

Sabine's compendium is one of the sources discussed by William Henry Egle, author of the 1896 book *Pennsylvania Genealogies*. "We are loath to dispel the halo which glimmers around the life of the celebrated grammarian," says Egle, who goes on to extinguish the halo's glow. Egle cites a letter of William

Darby, a Pennsylvania native who knew many of the Murray clan at the time of the Revolution. Darby contrasts Lindley with Lindley's cousin, Robert Dixon, "whose blood was the first Pennsylvania offering to the cause of Independence." Indeed, Darby accuses Lindley of taking sides "with the enemies of our country."[9]

Nevertheless, the myth of Lindley's noninvolvement proved hard to kill. When John Lindly, the Lindley family genealogist, wrote his book in 1924, he ignored the Darby letter altogether. "Egle," says Lindly of Lindley Murray, "seems disposed to class him as a loyalist, and states that Sabine so classes him, but does not cite any overt act of opposition to the patriotic cause by Murray."[10] Since the main purpose of the *Memoirs* is to cover up such instances of overt opposition, this is not surprising.

The fact that Lindley attempted to draw a veil over his conduct in the Revolution should not blind us to his real accomplishment, which was his textbooks. To fully understand them, particularly the *English Reader* and the Enlightenment philosophy it propounded, it is necessary to delve into the past of the Murray and Lindley families in America.

The Murrays and Lindleys of Pennsylvania

IN HIS *MEMOIRS*, LINDLEY TELLS US he was born "in the year 1745 in Swetara, near Lancaster, in the state of Pennsylvania." This was frontier country, and Lindley's identification is somewhat confusing in light of the geographical names used in the area today.

Swatara Creek (Swatara is today's spelling) rises in what is now Berks County and meanders for over 40 miles in a southwesterly direction to empty into the Susquehanna River about ten miles south of the state capital of Harrisburg and just north of the nuclear plant at Three Mile Island.

The creek passes from Berks County through Lebanon County and finally into Dauphin County. Along or near its path, it gives its name to several current geographic entities, including Swatara State Park and Swatara Gap in Lebanon County, as well as Swatara Township in Dauphin County, located where the creek flows into the river.

In 1745, Lebanon County and Dauphin County did not exist—they were part of Lancaster County. The town of Lancaster, then by far the most important settlement in the area, is about 25 miles from where Lindley was born. Today, the closest settlement to Lindley's birthplace, about a mile away, is the village of Harper Tavern, eighteen miles northeast of Harrisburg. Lindley was born near a mill owned by his father, which used the waters of Swatara Creek. To add to the confusion, Swatara Creek is today known locally as Indiantown Creek. (The name derives from an Indian village that was situated there, and is recalled in the name of the nearby Fort Indiantown Military Reservation.)

Lindley's father, Robert, came from a Scotch-Irish Presbyterian family. He had emigrated with his brother and his own father to Pennsylvania from Ireland in 1732. Robert's father, John, was a native of Perthshire, Scotland, who had emigrated to County Armagh, where his son was born. After arriving in Pennsylvania, John Murray bought over 200 acres of land on the Swatara Creek, then in Hanover Township, an agriculturally rich area. Robert Murray became proprietor of the family's prosperous mill on Swatara Creek while still in his teens.[1]

Mary Lindley, who would become Robert's wife and Lindley's mother, was the daughter of Thomas Lindley (1684–1743), who was also an immigrant. Thomas had been born into a Quaker family in the village of Ballincash in County Wicklow. He later moved to Ringsend, County Dublin, probably to pursue his trade of blacksmithing. He emigrated from there, arriving in Philadelphia about 1718.

Soon after coming to Philadelphia, Thomas applied to the Monthly Meeting in Dublin, Ireland, for clearness to marry. His bride was Hannah Durborow (also spelled Desbrough), daughter of a Philadelphia brewer, an occupation frequently followed by Quakers both in Britain and the colonies. One of Hannah's grandchildren would become known as a brewer in New York.

In the classic way of emigrant families, Thomas Lindley's brother had preceded him to the New World. James Lindley, Jr., six years older, had arrived in Pennsylvania in 1713, bringing documentation from the Quaker meeting in County Carlow, Ireland, to the Friends Meeting at Newark (now Kennett), in Chester County. James had married Eleanor Parke in Ireland in 1705; several of her relatives also emigrated to Pennsylvania around this time, eventually establishing themselves as one of the Commonwealth's leading families. Soon after his arrival, James had purchased 200 acres from William Penn, Jr., in the development at New Garden, Pennsylvania. In this deed, he is described as a yeoman, but when he buys 400 acres at London Grove in 1722, he is listed as a blacksmith. Perhaps James had picked up the trade from his younger brother in the intervening years. By the time James Lindley, Jr., died in 1740, he had a considerable estate. It included a thousand acres of land and personal property worth £1,115.

Thomas Lindley was also prospering. By 1724, he was well enough established to take on an indentured employee; for teaching him the blacksmith trade, he received from the young man's family a parcel of land in Philadelphia. Then in 1727, with a group of other Quakers, including some of the most prominent merchants in Philadelphia, Thomas Lindley became a founding owner of the Durham Furnace on the Delaware River in Bucks County. The plantation, initially covering almost 6,000 acres, contained "excellent iron ore and limestone" and became one of the leading forges in the colonies.[2]

The driving force behind the Durham purchase and its major stockholder was James Logan, the famous Philadelphia merchant and close ally of the Penn family. It is likely that Thomas Lindley was brought into the project as a technical expert because of his experience with iron—he is listed as an anchorsmith in the purchase agreement for the land. As an anchorsmith, of course, Thomas would have had experience with iron. In the normal course of his work, he would have been involved with the maritime merchants who were his Durham partners. He held a one-sixteenth share in the venture, which cost him less than £50 in Pennsylvania currency. Thomas's participation may also indicate that the partners looked to anchormaking as one source of sales for their iron production. Ownership of an iron ore forge—many Friends were connected with iron manufacture—was to reappear in the Murray family in the next generation.

Logan founded Durham Furnace in the wake of the 1724 reduction of the import duty on colonial pig iron shipped into Britain. The new duty per ton was less than four shillings compared to over two pounds for foreign countries. The action of Parliament was consistent with the British mercantile policy of making the colonies on the one hand a source of raw materials and on the other a market for finished manufactured goods. Logan targeted Britain as a major buyer of the Durham operation's iron. In 1728, from Durham's first production of pig iron, he shipped three tons to London, hoping to find a market. However, his plan seems to have foundered—Pennsylvania's exports of iron to Britain remained insignificant over the years after 1728. The domestic market had to suffice.[3]

Within a few years, Thomas Lindley seems to have shifted his attention from the Durham operation and looked west. About 1733, he took up residence in Lancaster County, buying 480 acres of land in Paxtang Township, a few miles from Robert Murray's residence in Swatara. Thomas Lindley, already a man of some importance, quickly became a member of the local elite. In 1738, he became a justice of the peace, and then served in the Pennsylvania Assembly from 1739 through 1743, the year he died. Thomas Lindley's influence must have been strong, because he was the leading vote-getter on the slate elected from Lancaster County in 1740.

In order to secure the country from Indian tribes, many of the residents of Lancaster County, particularly the Scotch-Irish immigrants, who had a reputation as pugnacious fighters, had been settled on their lands by the authorities without obtaining proper titles. Newly arrived Irish Quakers had also been settled there without deeds.

Politically, Thomas Lindley was a leader of the so-called anti-proprietary party, which defended the rights and liberties of frontier settlers in Lancaster County against the claims for compensation of the colony's "proprietors"—William Penn's heirs, to whom he had willed title to his lands. In this hotly contested battle, the provincial Quakers allied themselves with Scotch-Irish Presbyterian and German immigrants. It was not a difficult position for the Quakers to take. As Alan Tully, a historian of the conflict, says, "The majority of Quakers had always been among the stoutest defenders of popular freedoms, and they continued this tradition in Pennsylvania during the second quarter of the eighteenth century."[4]

The confrontation between the anti-proprietary party and William Penn's heirs, one of numerous similar struggles against the "establishment" and the crown throughout the colonies in the eighteenth century, helped create a climate of self-reliance and foster a taste for independence.

Thomas Lindley died in 1743. Robert Murray and Thomas's daughter Mary married in 1744. It was not the first marriage between the families. In the previous generation, Robert's uncle William, after his arrival in Pennsylvania in 1732, had married Mary Lindley's aunt Isabella. These family connections were a likely reason why Thomas Lindley had decided to buy land in Paxtang Township.[5]

Robert and Mary moved to Swatara after the marriage. Lindley Murray was born there the following year. (Later, the couple would have eleven more children, of whom four survived into adulthood in addition to Lindley).[6]

All his life, Robert Murray was a man who seized the main chance. His marriage to Mary Lindley, for which he abandoned his Presbyterian creed and converted to the Society of Friends, gave the young miller access to the top echelon of Pennsylvania's Quaker merchants, many of whom knew Thomas Lindley not only from his Philadelphia days, but also from serving with him in the Assembly.[7]

Perhaps Robert Murray was able to take advantage of Quaker solicitude in the wake of Thomas Lindley's death in 1743. In any case, from at least 1745 on, Robert Murray was operating as a merchant, making trading trips to the West Indies.[8] These early trips undoubtedly capitalized on Murray's position as a miller; flour and wheat were Pennsylvania's major exports to the West Indies.[9] From this point on, Robert Murray's allies in business would be almost exclusively his fellow Quakers.

The Spectacular Rise of Robert Murray in New York

3

IN THE EARLY 1750s, there was a significant movement of Quakers from Pennsylvania to new lands in North Carolina. Thomas Lindley's nephew (also called Thomas, a son of his older brother James) pulled up stakes in Pennsylvania and headed south.

It may be that Mary Lindley Murray, her husband Robert and their family accompanied her cousin to North Carolina. In the *Memoirs*, Lindley says his father believed "that some commercial advantage would attend a temporary residence in that province." The Murray family was in North Carolina in 1751 (the year Lindley records he was taken out of school in Philadelphia). Whether a business enterprise failed to take root or better prospects beckoned, Robert Murray left North Carolina in 1753 and moved to New York.

It was a shrewd choice. New York was on the verge of taking its place as one of the premier cities of the British Empire. The population, about 12,500 when Robert Murray arrived, continued to expand at a steady pace. And, as the intellectual historian Thomas Bender notes, "it is possible to identify the 1750s as the moment when New York City assumed self-consciousness as an eighteenth-century provincial city."[1]

Robert Murray was arriving in a city that already had an established, "old money" merchant and entrepreneurial elite. Its members ran family enterprises that frequently went back to the

15

early days of the colony, and had by marriage forged interlocking bonds with their peers. Families with familiar names such as the Van Cortlandts, Van Rensselaers, Livingstons, Bayards, De Lanceys, Beekmans, Roosevelts, Schuylers, Baches, Waltons, Alsops, Brevoorts, Goelets, Abeels, Lows, Harisons and Philipses, to name a few, were solidly established in business already and often had incomes from extensive landholdings as well.[2]

Robert Murray's status as a Quaker tended at first to separate him from this commercial elite, but it also provided natural allies from among fellow Friends. As Hugh Barbour and J. William Frost note in *The Quakers*: "By the mid-eighteenth century, Quakers had become almost a clan of extended kinfolk bound together by patterns of commerce and religion."

In New York, these Friends mainly operated on a somewhat lower commercial level than the long-established families. A few, however, had gained commercial prominence. The most important were Walter and Samuel Franklin. In 1764, the Franklins had interests in six vessels, more than any other New York merchants; in addition, they kept a portion of their capital invested in marine insurance. On a secondary economic plane among the Quakers were merchants such as the Bownes and the trading and store-owning Delaplaines, with whom the Murrays also did business.[3]

As he began his siege of New York, Robert had in his favor an economic boom. From 1754 on, the colonies were involved in the Seven Years' War between Britain and France. New York became the main entrepôt for shipment of goods to Canada, where much of the fighting was taking place, enriching those New York merchants involved in transatlantic trade. From 1754 to 1759, the customs value of English manufactures imported from London to New York rose from £87,499 to £483,952, a figure not matched throughout the rest of the colonial period.[4]

This boom made Robert Murray's fortune—his rise was phenomenal. In little more than a decade and a half, this enterprising, hard-working man was making money from an array of businesses. Even in an era when merchants typically had fingers in many pies, Robert's investments were extremely varied. His activities follow the general pattern identified by Thomas C. Cochran: "The large seaport merchant of the mid-eighteenth century imported and exported, transported and warehoused, sold wholesale and retail, lent money and arranged for investments, and both sought and subscribed to insurance."[5]

The most important of Robert Murray's businesses was the substantial shipping tonnage that he owned—three vessels and an interest in a fourth by 1764. As an adjunct to this, he interested himself in whaling, fitting out a sloop with the Franklins that sailed from New York port in April 1768, a venture that led a local newspaper, the *New York Mercury*, to hope for a revival of the "neglected" whaling business in the city.[6]

Another of Murray's key businesses was his wharf, strategically placed on the lower East River at Wall Street. Such ownership implied that he also acted as a freight forwarder. Robert had purchased the land for the wharf from Cornelius Law in 1766. Without bothering to obtain permission of the Common Council, he immediately went to work on laying the foundations of the pier. When objections arose, he persuaded some citizens to petition the Council to let the work continue on the grounds that it would be "more convenient to the publick than if the same had not been made." Thus the Council approved, retrospectively, a 25-foot-wide pier with space below for the tide to pass through and with a bridge over it for the use of carriages.[7]

Murray's wharf was an active scene of commerce for many years afterwards, and played a role in numerous future historical events. It was the scene in 1774, for example, of the "New York Tea Party," where citizens opposed to importation of British goods threw cases of tea overboard. And at the end of the ensuing Revolution, it was at Murray's wharf that George Washington debarked on his way to being sworn in as the first President. Robert lived near his wharf, on Queen Street (now Pearl), at the corner of Beekman Street.

In addition to his shipping enterprises, Robert was an extremely competitive figure in the marine insurance business. In 1764, for example, the normal insurance premium for voyages between New York and London was 2 to 3 percent of the value of the cargo. But Murray was undercutting his competitors with a rate of 1.5 percent. Robert dealt in indigo with the Delaplaines, and sold imported goods from the store of Murray and Pearsall on the waterfront. His partner in the store, Thomas Pearsall, was a relative of the Franklins. Thomas and his wife Freelove Pearsall were, of course, Quakers.[8]

In the late 1750s, New York consumers were enjoying newly introduced commodities, and items once thought to be luxuries were coming within the purchasing power of ordinary citizens. According to New York newspaper advertisements, Murray and Pearsall sold "for ready Money or short credit" a wide assortment of goods from nails and window glass to worsted and velvet, as well as Cheshire cheese, English tea, clocks and "neat silver watches." In a hint of what was to come in the Murray family, the store also offered "primmers, spelling books, testaments, young mans companions." "Companions" were required reading for young clerks aspiring to make their way in New York's expanding mercantile world—they gave advice on matters such as letter-writing, arithmetic, bookkeeping, calculating interest, and showed proper forms for legal documents such as indentures and bonds.[9]

One reason for the wide array of stock offered by many New York stores was the lack of liquidity throughout most of the eighteenth century. With little cash available, and no banking system to promote lending, merchants had to do some business by barter, and so needed to carry a varied stock. When Murray and Pearsall advertised goods for "Ready money," they were addressing the problem of cash flow.[10]

Although he was certainly affluent and an important member of New York's business elite, Robert's position has often been exaggerated by commentators. Based on little or no evidence, Robert has been characterized as New York's leading merchant of the time. This judgment appears to be based on his notoriety rather than reality, on Robert's widespread business interests, his lavish lifestyle and the continuation of the Murray family as prominent New York business people over several generations. The renown of Lindley Murray and the legend of Mary Lindley Murray's role in the Battle of Manhattan also contributed to subsequent exaggeration of Robert Murray's place among New York's businessmen.[11]

In addition to his immigrant roots, a situation that often spurs anxiety, and to a possible history of business failure in North Carolina, Robert Murray simply lacked the extensive family and business interconnections developed over the decades by New York's old-money elite. Such connections were not merely a matter of social pride. In an economy that was continually hampered by lack of specie, family connections provided a reservoir of potential capital for investments and for loans in time of trouble. Robert's Quaker allies could be of help in this area, but they could not match the close and longstanding relationships of the older families.

Robert's main business—shipping and overseas trade—was an intrinsically unstable and insecure one. The risk of losing ships and cargoes was normally spread among several investors and buffered by marine insurance, but this reduced profitability. In colonial times, most merchant houses were partnerships, generally of two to four owners. The owners tended to be members of the same family, such as the Franklins, the Crugers and the Waltons, but the partnership did help spread losses. Robert Murray, however, worked alone in his early years in New York, which also made his situation more parlous. Several years after his arrival in New York, Robert was joined in business by his brother John, who was almost two decades younger. John did not become a partner for some years and always had a junior status until after the Revolution.[12]

Among the generations of Murrays, there was a continuing insecurity about their business affairs that sometimes amounted almost to desperation. This anxiety is evident in Robert, the immigrant boy, but is equally well developed in his cosseted, well-educated son Lindley. Despite their apparent wealth, their energy and their business acumen, the first two generations of New York Murrays, spurred by money concerns, often made unwise decisions at moments of crisis.

Robert's business situation made his Quaker links all the more important, and he assiduously cultivated them. An early instance of this sort of networking occurs in 1755, when Robert joined with "some Friends" to help William Palmer, who was too sick to provide for his family. Robert contributed a pound, and his partner Thomas Pearsall ten shillings, to the fund, an indication (in addition to the firm's name) that Robert—in a pattern he was to follow throughout his life—was the dominant partner in the store.[13] In 1759, Robert became a member of the New York Meeting for Sufferings, the important standing committee that handled the business of the New York Quaker Meeting between larger sessions.[14] (Its name derived from the time when much of its business related to helping relieve the sufferings of persecuted Friends; it is today known as the Representative Meeting.)

As is usual with the sort of economic boom that happened soon after Robert's arrival in New York, there was a spurt of building in its wake, in which Robert Murray participated. From the 1750s through the early 1760s, many prominent New York merchant families constructed homes north of what was then the city—"literally dozens of lovely seats."[15]

Robert Murray's estate was one of the finest of these seats. Inclenberg was located a few hundred yards west of the important north–south route, the Boston Post Road (also known as the Kingsbridge Road), approximately the route of Lexington Avenue today (but which at the time proceeded along the Bowery and to the southern tip of the island). Just to the west of the Murray property (towards the Hudson River) was another main north–south route, the Bloomingdale Road. Among the Murray neighbors was James Duane, later mayor of New York. His estate

Gramercy, today the neighborhood surrounding Gramercy Park, was about three-quarters of a mile south of Robert Murray's Inclenberg.[16]

A magnificent place altogether was Inclenberg, approached by an avenue of magnolias, elms, spruce and Lombardy poplars, which led to a wide lawn bordered on either side by extensive gardens. The spacious, two-story mansion had a broad veranda extending around three sides, and the front windows command-ed a view over Kip's Bay and the East River. Inclenberg was fre-quently spoken of by chroniclers as one of the loveliest spots on the island.[17]

In addition to building this impressive house, Robert Murray displayed his wealth in other ways. He drove about the city in a luxurious coach. Its interior was decorated with eighteen yards of broad lace, 40 yards of common lace, eleven yards of silk bom-bazel, with fife tassels and worsted tufting. The coach cost the enormous sum of £153 14s. Robert was apparently sensitive about criticism—some of it from fellow Friends—about his lifestyle and aristocratic ways, so he took to calling this lavish coach, with con-summate hypocrisy, his "leathern conveniency."[18]

Robert Murray's contacts in Philadelphia may have provided models for his business practices and lavish lifestyle. One Philadelphia Friend, Israel Pemberton, a partner with Thomas Lindley in the Durham Forge and fellow Assemblyman, seems to have been a model, and very likely a business contact, for Robert. As Frederick Tolles says, Pemberton was "a great trader, whose ships were seen in most of the major Atlantic ports." It may have been from the example of Pemberton that Robert Murray learned that shipowning was a road to substantial wealth.[19] The Pembertons and the Murrays remained close friends and allies through the next generation.

Another Durham Forge partner seems to have been a model for Robert Murray in another way—how to spend the money he earned. The very rich Anthony Morris II (whose brother William served in the Pennsylvania Assembly with Thomas Lindley) lived in a luxurious style that scandalized many of those devoted to the simple life advocated by the Friends.[20] It is reminiscent of the similar outcry against Robert Murray's lifestyle in New York City many years later.

Along with the splendor that Robert Murray loved came other things we normally associate with this kind of life. The Murrays were renowned as hosts. They "entertained at various times almost every foreigner of distinction who came to American shores, and it was rare for such to visit New York without letters of introduction" to Robert Murray. One of the most colorful of such entertainments, remembered in a family letter and described a century later in a book by Sarah Murray, a descendant, was the *fête champêtre* for 30 guests given by the Murrays in honor of the Tunisian Ambassador. The Ambassador, who sported a turban and an eight-inch-long beard, was clad in a silk jacket over which was a dark blue robe richly embroidered in gold.[21]

If the world came to the Murrays' table, so must travelers from within America, as well as the notables of New York itself. In eighteenth-century New York, the intellectual historian Thomas Bender accurately remarks, "practical men of affairs and the literati were intimate" and "intellectual life was founded on conversation."[22] This is the environment in which Lindley Murray grew to young manhood. He was a wealthy and privileged youth, the scion of a rich family, from a home that welcomed international travelers. As the oldest son, Lindley was undoubtedly present as the affairs of the day and the latest ideas from Europe were discussed at the dining tables and in the receiving rooms of Inclenberg.

The Enlightenment Education of Lindley Murray

THE EDUCATION OF LINDLEY MURRAY provides a casebook for examining the way children of the American mercantile gentry were brought up in the 1750s and 1760s. Perhaps even more important, it shows how the eighteenth century's pervasive, if often veiled, Enlightenment ideas affected the education of one individual.

According to Lindley in the *Memoirs*, part of his early education was at the famous Academy and Charitable School in the Province of Pennsylvania, founded by Benjamin Franklin. Lindley left Swatara to take advantage of it. "About my sixth or seventh year," he says, "I was sent to the city of Philadelphia, that I might have the advantage of a better school than the country afforded. I well remember being some time at the academy of Philadelphia, the English department of which was then conducted by the truly respectable Ebeneezer Kinnersley." Lindley was a pupil there only for a short time, however. He was taken out of the school to accompany his family when they went to North Carolina later in the year.[1]

The Academy had opened its doors on January 7, 1751. Franklin had first floated the idea of the Academy in 1743, but no action was taken until after he published in 1749 his "Proposals Relating to the Education of Youth in Pennsylvania." Then Franklin and a group of friends opened a public subscription to establish the school. Franklin shrewdly asked 24 of the largest subscribers to serve as trustees. They were of course among the richest and most powerful men in Pennsylvania. Their support not only insured a sound continuing financial basis for the school, but their prestige produced both instant respectability and wide publicity.[2]

It is worth noting that Robert Murray chose to send Lindley to this fashionable new school rather than Philadelphia's best-known and well-established Quaker institution, the William Penn Charter School. It is an early indication of a tendency that Robert would follow throughout his life—he often gave more weight to the fashions and lifestyles of the worldly Philadelphia merchants than the strict path of his more observant Quaker brethren. It had proven true of his lavish life in New York as well as his choice of school for Lindley.

Lindley could have been a pupil when Franklin's school opened its doors in January 1751, or possibly he began to attend after his sixth birthday in April. In any case, it indicates he may have been a somewhat precocious child. Though a goodly number of children began a master's school at six, the normal age for starting was seven.

A child like Lindley, from a prosperous family, would have learned to read before he ever went to a formal school such as the Philadelphia academy. Most children at this time learned their letters either at home at their mother's knee, or at a dame school kept by a local woman. Children began to attend dame schools as early as age three. The teacher—mother or dame—would read out the letters of the alphabet and basic syllables from a book such as *The New England Primer*; the student would look at the letters in the book and repeat them.

While discussing the academy, Lindley says he remembers reading and enjoying *The Travels of Cyrus*, a popular and widely available book in the colonies at the time. In addition—an important milestone for the future grammarian—he recalls being "agreeably exercised in the business of parsing sentences."[3]

Lindley does not comment on his education in North Carolina from 1751 to 1753, but after Robert Murray got to New York in 1753, Lindley tells us he was placed by his father "at a good school, in which I made the usual progress of young learners." One of the things Lindley learned at the New York school was writing. His description of what it was like to be a penmanship student (which he brings up in the *Memoirs* immediately after his discussion of the family's arrival in New York) is remarkable, and perhaps the best contemporary account we have of such training. It is well worth quoting:

> About this period, a very happy impression was made on my mind, by a piece which was given me to write, and in the performance of which I had to exhibit a specimen of my best handwriting. The sheet was decorated round its edges with a number of pleasing figures, displayed with taste and simplicity. In the centre my performance was to be contained. This was a transcript of the visit and salutation of the angels to the shepherds, near Bethlehem, who were tending their flocks by night. The beauty of the sheet; the property I was to have in it; and the distinction which I expected from performing the work in a handsome manner; prepared my mind for relishing the solemn narrative, and the interesting language of the angels to the shepherds. I was highly pleased with the whole.[4]

The fact that Lindley only had to fill in the center of an already prepared sheet indicates that this exercise was done when he was fairly young. But his enthusiasm for penmanship shines through, so it should come as no surprise that throughout his life, until his death at 81, Lindley wrote a remarkably clear, confident hand. It was an important accomplishment for a young man destined for the merchant's life. The comparison is evident, for example, when the researcher matches Lindley's handwriting with that of his contemporary and acquaintance John Jay. Jay had an impeccable university education at King's College (later Columbia College) in New York, but in comparison to Lindley's fluent and clear hand, Jay's writing is somewhat crabbed and difficult to decipher.

The end of Lindley's formal education apparently came with another stint at Franklin's Philadelphia academy, in 1756–57. It seems to have been a kind of finishing-school year, intended to be the end of formal studies. It provided an opportunity not only to study at the prestigious school, but to spend time among the wealthy merchant families of Philadelphia, the intellectual and social center of American Quakerism. In addition, Philadelphia was home to numerous relatives and family friends of the Lindleys and Murrays.

Lindley does not specifically mention this second spell in Philadelphia in the *Memoirs*. At the time when he was writing about his early education, he was recalling events of more than a half-century before. His memory about these events is fairly good, but his account does pose problems concerning dates. He cannot be right about Ebeneezer Kinnersley being his teacher in 1751, for example.

Kinnersley joined the faculty (as head of its English school) only in 1753, after Lindley's departure for North Carolina. However, the academy lists Lindley as a student in 1756, and this is the likely source of Lindley's memory of Kinnersley, as well as of his reading of the fairly advanced *Travels of Cyrus*. Parsing sentences is also something that would have taken place at a time later than a child's first year at a master's school like the academy, so this memory could also date from the second spell at the academy.[5]

As the oldest son of the family, Lindley was slated to succeed his father in the Murrays' merchant business. The first step in that process was record keeping. "At an early age," Lindley tells us, "I was placed in the counting house of my father, who was desirous of my entering the mercantile profession." This counting house work began at some point after 1756, following the completion of his year at the Philadelphia academy. Lindley was now eleven, "an early age" indeed.

However, the drudgery of the counting house did not appeal in the least to Lindley. He soon grew resentful at "the strictness with which I was kept to business, and the undue restraints as I conceived, which were put, at that early period, on my lively spirits and allowable indulgences. . . I wished to be anything but a merchant." But Robert was resolved to turn his son towards commerce. "My father kept steady to his purpose," Lindley tells us. "He probably thought that my dislike to the business world would, in time, abate."[6]

In an attempt to reconcile Lindley to the merchant's profession (and undoubtedly reflecting his son's attraction to the stimulations of the City of Brotherly Love), Robert once again sent Lindley to Philadelphia, this time for a year's work in the counting house of the prominent Quaker merchant Robert Waln. (Waln and his family are best known to historians today as characters in the diary of their Philadelphia neighbor, Elizabeth Drinker.) Lindley says his father was "influenced, perhaps, by a hope, that residence with a merchant at a distance from home, would better reconcile me to the employment." The date of the certification of Lindley's apprenticeship is in the records of the Friends' Philadelphia Monthly Meeting—December 3, 1761.[7]

In the Charles Roberts Autograph Collection at the library of Haverford College is an inch-and-a-half high piece of paper that reads as follows: "Receiv'd March 5th 1762 of Thomas Riche Seventeen pounds four shillings & Ninepence in full for Robert Waln. Lindley Murray." The cutting is an account book entry, saved not for its own sake but because it bears the autograph of the famous textbook writer Lindley Murray. The sliver of paper not only establishes that Robert Waln was Lindley's employer during his apprenticeship year, but indicates the kind of work the fifteen-year-old was doing. It is the dreary Bob Cratchit labor of the counting house clerk, inscribing in the merchant's account book, day after day, dozens of such entries. It is easy to see how such work would have irked an intellectually adventurous young man like Lindley.[8]

The Philadelphia apprenticeship failed to reconcile Lindley to the life of the merchant, and Robert acknowledged it—"this expedient did not answer his [Robert's] expectations; and, after some time, he consented to my return to New-York." When Lindley came back, though, the sixteen-year-old once again gave assistance to his father "in the routine of his commercial affairs."

Robert kept the young man firmly under his thumb. "Though my father," Lindley says, "had an earnest desire to promote my interest and happiness, yet he appeared to me, in some respects, rather too rigorous." One of his father's rules was that Lindley should never leave the house in the evenings without his father's permission. Lindley's troubles with Robert came to a head one day when his father was absent from home and Lindley accepted an invitation from his Uncle John Murray. Robert took this to be a breach of the rules and Lindley tells us he "received a very severe chastisement; and was threatened with a repetition of it for any similar offense."

Lindley was outraged at the unfairness of it all, and the clash emboldened him to leave home, though not until he had a new suit of clothes made for himself—he seems to have had adequate monetary resources to carry out his plan. "Taking my books and all my property with me," he removed himself to a "seminary" in Burlington, New Jersey (undoubtedly the well-known Quaker Academy there) with the purpose of learning French.[9]

Lindley Murray tells this story in the *Memoirs* five decades later. He says the confrontation took place when he was "about fourteen years of age." Since Lindley places the incident after his return from his Philadelphia apprenticeship, however, he would have been sixteen. That confusion is minor. More problematic is Lindley's telling of the story from this point on.

For example, though Lindley does not say so, if he had not already been made aware of the situation, the master of the Burlington academy must immediately have ascertained who this young man arriving on his doorstep was. Robert Murray was one of the best-known Friends in the colonies. The master certainly would have wasted no time in contacting the family, and would never have countenanced Lindley's continuing as a student without Robert Murray's acquiescence. So it was not exactly a case of running away.

Lindley acknowledges that his family knew where he was—"soon after I had left home, inquiries were made to discover the place to which I had retreated... but I had made up my mind not to return, and subject myself again to a treatment which I had felt to be improper and unmerited."

Another problem with Lindley's narrative is his account of how he returned "to the paternal roof." According to him, he met on a trip to Philadelphia "a gentleman who had some time before dined at my father's house." This man just happened to be carrying a letter to someone in New York, and claiming he had just missed the last mail, "he begged that I would deliver it with my own hand, as soon as I arrived in New York." Says Lindley: "Surprised by his request, and unwilling to state to him my situation, I engaged to take good care of the letter."

Though he had intended to return from Philadelphia to his school in Burlington, Lindley says his "tacit engagement" to deliver the letter in person "operated so powerfully on my mind, that after I had rode a few miles, I determined, whatever risk and expense I might incur, to hire a carriage for the purpose, to go to New York as speedily as possible, deliver the letter, and return as speedily as possible." Lindley delivered the letter, but had to remain in the city overnight to await the morning sailing of the packet boat to New Jersey.

At the inn where he was staying, he just happened to be recognized by someone he knew. Subsequently, his Uncle John called on him at the inn, and urged Lindley to go with him to his father's house. Lindley refused, but John pressed him, pointing out the distress that he had caused his mother by his absence. This argument touched Lindley, and he agreed to see his mother. He was having a "truly affecting" visit with her when his father "unexpectedly" came in. "He saluted me very tenderly; and expressed great satisfaction on seeing me again. Every degree of resentment was immediately dissipated."

Lindley tells all of this in the *Memoirs* without the least acknowledgement that the sequence is filled with unlikely coincidences. What is really going on in this tale? First, Lindley seems intent on constructing a narrative that preserves and underlines the serious nature of his break with his father. What the story of the clash accomplishes—and from its lengthy treatment in the book we can sense its importance to the author—is to emphasize Lindley's differences with Robert. And the most obvious reason behind that emphasis is to retroactively and symbolically separate himself from his father's political loyalism, and, perhaps unconsciously, to evoke from the perspective of 1809 the unfairness of his father's treatment of him at the end of the Revolution.[10]

But to continue the story. As part of the new harmony in the family, Lindley requested and received "a private tutor to instruct me in classical knowledge and liberal studies," including science. Lindley is modest about what the tutoring accomplished, but does say it helped "improve my taste, and increase my desire, for learning and knowledge." At the same time, Lindley undertook a campaign to finally free himself of the merchant's life. "As my mind improved, and my views enlarged, I became still more attached to literary pursuits; I wished for a profession connected with these pursuits; and the study of law attracted my attention." Lindley's connection of literary pursuits with law may strike some today as odd. But in the colonial context, it was perfectly logical. There was no way for a strictly literary person to make a living. Lawyers filled the role of the literati; they were at the heart of the intellectual and literary elite.[11]

At first, Robert discouraged Lindley's ambition, arguing that a merchant could make much more money than a lawyer. But Lindley continued to pursue his goal and wrote a letter to Robert making his case. The letter came to the attention of Robert's legal counselor, the eminent lawyer Benjamin Kissam (c. 1732–1780), who became an advocate of Lindley's cause. Finally, Robert consented, paying Kissam a "considerable sum of money" for training Lindley in the law. The fee was no doubt the same amount specified in the rules of the New York bar published the following year—£200. That was the amount that Kissam charged Peter Jay when his son John Jay, later a leading patriot and the first Chief Justice of the United States, became a clerk in the Kissam firm after his graduation from King's College. Lindley began studying for the bar at Kissam's office, located in the fashionable neighborhood of Golden Hill (around today's John and Gold Streets) in 1763. He was eighteen. He got in just under the wire. In January 1764, the new rules of the New York bar required two years of study at a university as well a clerkship fee of £200.[12]

Once he had relented, Robert Murray tried to see to it that Lindley had the best possible chance to succeed in the law. "After some time," Lindley tells us, Robert "very generously presented me with an excellent library, which comprehended both books of law, and some parts of general literature." In fact, though Robert had fought Lindley's decision, it was a common thing for the leading families to have at least one son in the legal profession. At a time when there were comparatively few mechanisms of support for business, family solidarity was of utmost importance. When the firm's lawyer was also a family member, loyalty—and secrecy about business affairs—was almost assured. Lindley Murray maintained that loyalty. His ability to offer legal advice to his family, which he did frequently until the end of his life, only deepened the ties.[13]

If Lindley thought, however, that a law clerkship would free him from the drudgery he associated with the counting house, he was mistaken. "I cannot, however, say that I always found the study of law to be pleasant," he admits in the *Memoirs*. Years before, in a newspaper article in 1745, William Livingston (who was to become John Jay's father-in-law) had railed against the clerkship system, which brought attorneys large sums—

"unmerited money, God knows"—and subjected the young clerks to a life that was "scandalous, horrid, base, and infamous to the last Degree." Added Livingston: "To make a young Fellow trifle away the Bloom of his Age, when his Invention is readiest, his Imagination warmest, and all his Faculties in full Vigour and Maturity, is a servile Drudgery. . . and fit only for a Slave."[14]

Even with the growing number of legal forms available, there was much laborious writing to be done, including transcription of pleadings and judgement rolls. It was hardly better in Lindley's second year at Kissam's, though the newly arrived John Jay had taken over the scut work. Lindley, now senior clerk, kept Kissam's registers, billed clients, and handled trial preparation matters. The work and related study included, Lindley noted dourly, "many barren and uninviting tracts, and extensive fields of laborious employment." Still Lindley persevered, finished his legal studies, and entered practice in 1767, at about the age of 22.[15]

After being admitted to the bar, Lindley and Jay continued an acquaintance throughout their lives, though the relationship was severely strained by the events leading up to the Revolution and by the conflict itself. One activity that united Lindley, Jay and other bright young men was membership in The Debating Club, a group that typified the Enlightenment style. Its members included Murray, Jay, James De Lancey, John Bard, Peter Van Shaack, William Laight, Egbert Benson and John Vardill. Though a dozen years older than the younger debaters, Samuel Kissam was also a member. They met on Thursdays at "Mrs. Brass's" at six and continued till ten, sometimes till midnight.

With Peter Van Shaack serving as secretary, the debate topic one night was: "Was Virginius morally justified in putting his daughter, Virginia, to death to preserve her violation by Appius?" Arguing the affirmative, Kissam maintained that the laws of Rome gave unlimited power to parents where their children were concerned. They could sell them or even kill them. Lindley, arguing the negative, said that the legal power vested in parents applied only to cases of disobedience or fault, and that it was absurd to mete out a punishment when there had been no crime. Every person had a right to existence, Murray said, and could not be deprived of it except through crimes or by proper and lawful means.[16]

To a certain extent, the substance of the debate echoed the kinds of political issues regarding the powers of monarchical government that were in the haunted air and which would divide the members of The Debating Club—some of whom would become patriots and others loyalists—in the years to come. Of course, in formal debates of this sort the speakers were not really expected to believe in the positions they upheld, merely (like good lawyers) to argue them with cogency and persuasiveness. But Lindley's argument certainly reflects the Enlightenment turn of mind he would display in his future writings. It may also have reflected the outrage at injustice he had felt in his clash with his father.[17]

2

A REVIEW OF THE PROCESS of Lindley Murray's education reveals much about how Enlightenment ideas influenced the young, especially those with intellectual ambitions. Their effect can be seen, for example, in Lindley's laudatory reference in the *Memoirs* to *The Travels of Cyrus*. This was one of the most popular books of the early Enlightenment. Its author was Andrew Michael Ramsay, born in 1686 in Ayr, Scotland, the son of a Calvinist baker. Ramsay became a Roman Catholic, served as secretary to the famous Archbishop Fénelon in France, and later became a Freemason and Deist.

The book was first published in France in 1727 as *Les Voyages de Cyrus*, with the English translation appearing the same year. The book went through more than 30 editions in English and French, and there were translations into German, Italian, Spanish and Greek. It remained popular into the early nineteenth century. The first American edition, based on the tenth English one, did not appear until 1793.

The Travels of Cyrus, described by Ramsay as a philosophical history, tells the story of Cyrus, heir to the throne of Persia, who visits Egypt, Greece, Crete, Tyre and Babylon and holds discussions on the philosophical beliefs in those places. The book raises questions that were to concern Lindley all his life. Cyrus finds worth in all the various beliefs and religions he encounters. This emphasis on the value of all religions is an obvious reaction to the legacy of viciously partisan religious wars that occupied much of the seventeenth century, and to the doctrines of Calvinism and Jansenism, both of which Ramsay knew at first hand. In the book, education is portrayed as a spiritual and moral journey, not an accumulation of facts; its purpose is to make the educated person an adherent of the highest principles and devoted to concern for others, not himself.

The Travels of Cyrus, available in imported editions, was obviously considered suitable fare for youngsters and girls in Philadelphia at the time Lindley was attending school there. The Quaker schoolmaster Robert Willan had ordered a copy of *The Travels of Cyrus* from a bookseller in 1751 for the use of his students. Another Philadelphia teacher, the esteemed Anthony Benezet, ordered a copy for his Quaker girls' school in 1754 or 1755.[18]

Throughout the *Memoirs* and in his correspondence, Lindley refers to the importance of a "liberal education." This concept, which includes the development of a mind furnished with an understanding of history, literature and science, differs from the Scholastic model that lasted from the Middle Ages through the first century of the American colonies. (In Lindley's view, liberal education would result in an openness of mind that resembled the one achieved by the hero of *The Travels of Cyrus*).

This theory of education, with its overtones of gentlemanly cultivation, and its assertion that education should not be merely a preparation for the church or other professions but rather the necessary basis for a thoughtful life, is a product of the Enlightenment. It was an ideal that Lindley hewed to throughout his life.

Lindley's ideas about liberal education appear early in the opening letter of the *Memoirs*. "My father did not possess the advantages of a liberal education," Lindley says, "by which his talents and virtues might have been still more extensively useful." For Lindley, such an education was not an ivory tower exercise, but the means of integrating an understanding of history, literature and science with a life of virtuous action in the world.

Lindley's own realization of his intense desire to be liberally educated dates from around the time of his return from his Philadelphia apprenticeship. "About this period," he says immediately after discussing his Philadelphia experience, "I contracted a taste for reading, and for a greater degree of literary improvement. The pleasures of study, and the advantages and distinctions, which learning and knowledge conferred upon individuals who fell under my observation, augmented my wishes for the acquisition of science and literature."[19]

Note the curious phraseology with which Lindley characterizes the type of knowledge he desired: "the acquisition of science and literature." To understand the context here, we must take a closer look at American intellectual life in the late 1750s, and the key role of Philadelphia in it. As the historian Andrew Hook has put it: "Given its intellectual preeminence, Philadelphia could not be other than the major transatlantic recipient of the exciting configuration of ideas that constituted the eighteenth-century Enlightenment in Europe."[20]

Philadelphia was the center of the American Enlightenment, and the driving force behind the nurture and propagation of Enlightenment ideas was the city's wealthiest and most socially prominent group, the Quaker merchant establishment. Several directors of Franklin's original Library Company (1746) were Quakers, as were almost half the members. Indeed, Pennsylvania's Friends contributed to the Enlightenment one of its best-known international symbols—the Good Quaker. Because of his family history, and Robert Murray's success in New York, Lindley Murray was closely linked to this class, and it is easy to see from Lindley Murray's early life what a magnet Philadelphia was for him. And Lindley was certainly not too young to begin absorbing the Enlightenment ideas blooming in Philadelphia—at that time boys regularly went to Harvard or Yale when they were 12 or 13.[21]

During the 1750s when Murray was resident at the Franklin academy and with Robert Waln, science was the rage in Philadelphia. Franklin, a close friend of many Quakers, and his colleagues (including Ebeneezer Kinnersley) had conducted in the 1740s and 1750s experiments in electricity, including the development of the lightning rod, that had set the whole world abuzz. They were the talk of the educated people of the town. In a textbook published over four decades after his Philadelphia experience, the *Sequel to the English Reader* (1802), Murray includes a selection from Franklin, and in the short account of Franklin that Murray prepared for his biographical appendix to the *Sequel*, he specifically mentions Franklin's writings on electricity, as well as on meteorology and mechanics.[22]

Another branch of science important to Lindley was medicine. Philadelphia was on the point of becoming the leader in America in medical education. In 1762, the year that Lindley was completing his apprenticeship at Robert Waln's, William Shippen of Philadelphia, who was to become an important figure in the city's medical schooling, returned from studying at the University of Edinburgh's famous medical school. In the same year, John Morgan, another Philadelphian studying at Edinburgh, was drawing up plans for what was to become the College of Philadelphia's medical school, which opened its doors in 1765. The romance of medicine was in the air and, indeed, Lindley Murray gave consideration to pursuing a medical career.[23]

So Lindley's phrase, "the acquisition of science and literature," seems a clear reflection of the influence of Philadelphia on this observant and intellectually ambitious young man.

The strong desire to learn French, evident in Lindley's break with his father and his decision to leave New York for the

Burlington seminary, also points to Enlightenment influences. "Here I purposed to remain," he says of his flight to the school in Burlington, "till I had learned the French language, which I thought would be of great use to me."[24] Why this desire to learn French? We can piece together an answer to this question by once again examining the practices of the Philadelphia Quaker elite and by looking at what was happening in the larger intellectual world at this time.

According to Frederick Tolles, in his book on the eighteenth century Philadelphia Quaker establishment, "knowledge of French was regarded as a desirable acquirement for the children of Quaker aristocrats." For example, he says, describing a leading family, "Isaac Norris II began studying French in his late teens; his father lent him encouragement by pointing out that whatever he acquired beyond a superficial acquaintance with languages would be both 'advantage and Ornament' to him." In 1742, Tolles points out, Philadelphia's Quakers had employed Anthony Benezet "to teach French in the English School under the care of the Monthly Meeting; undoubtedly he also included this subject in the curriculum of the Girls' school where he taught after 1754."[25]

But there is another likely reason, in addition to its social advantages, for Lindley Murray's decision to study French. In the very years when he was deciding to embrace the life of the mind, the French Enlightenment was at its height, and was the talk of literate circles in the great cities of Europe and America. It was the sort of subject that must have been frequently discussed with foreign visitors at the dinner table of Inclenberg.

The French Enlightenment had put forward the idea that science and the scientific cast of mind should be part of the intellectual equipment of any serious person. Scientists and popularizers of scientific ideas such as Fontenelle, Pluche, Réaumur, Buffon and Linnaeus had gained worldwide reputations with publications over the previous three decades. And reverence for science was being popularized throughout the literate world by the *Encyclopédie*, which had begun publishing its volumes in 1751.

As Henry May says in his book *The Enlightenment in America*: "A whole new and specifically French stage of the Enlightenment began with the publication of the first volumes of the *Encyclopédie* and the emergence in the dangerous daylight of a new circle of philosophes, whose opinions, witticisms, and intellectual style were imitated from St. Petersburg to London, from Berlin to Naples." And one might easily add, in Philadelphia and New York.[26]

Yet another reason why Murray wished to learn French may have been to read Voltaire. Not only was Voltaire the very epitome of the French Enlightenment, whose name was on the lips of every educated person while Murray was coming to intellectual maturity, but Voltaire was also a great admirer of the Society of Friends. Voltaire had been exiled in England from 1726 to 1728 and had become acquainted with the Quakers. In his *Letters Concerning the English Nation*, published in 1733, he devotes the book's first four letters to the Friends, praising members lavishly as modest, tolerant, rational speakers of the truth, and exemplars of the kind of Deism that Voltaire was promoting in opposition to traditional Christian theology. Whatever the truth of his contention, it cannot but have piqued Lindley Murray's imagination. The works of Voltaire were available in New York during Lindley's young manhood. The bookseller Garrat Noel advertised for sale in Weyman's *New York Gazette* on October 29, 1759, "Voltaire's Works, 6 vols." and "Candid [sic] by Voltaire."[27]

Indeed, there is evidence that Murray was well acquainted with Voltaire and respected his opinions. One need only look at the appendix of Lindley's French-language textbook, *Lecteur François*, where he provides short biographies of his contributors, to see how frequently he uses Voltaire's opinions on the writers. While he drew the line at including the controversial Voltaire himself in the *Lecteur François*, the book reflects Voltaire's taste and uses many of the authors most admired by French Enlightenment writers.[28]

So in seeking to acquire "science" as well as literature, Lindley Murray, the budding intellectual, was striving to become a man of his age, a man of the Enlightenment. And in learning French, he was not only acquiring an asset in the formation of a gentleman, but learning something that he felt gave him greater access to this Enlightenment world of science and literature.

Thus, in 1802, when his other textbooks were beginning to take off in both Britain and the United States—a moment when his printers would likely have gratefully accepted any book he wished to produce—Murray issued two readers in the French language. The books are a homage to the language he sacrificed to learn, but also to the Enlightenment scientific figures he admired. Murray put his knowledge of French and admiration for science to use, for example, by including selections from Fontenelle and Buffon in his *Lecteur François*, and from Pluche's *Spectacle de la Nature* in both his *Lecteur François* and his *Introduction au Lecteur François*.[29]

There was another aspect to Lindley's Enlightenment education. Educated people of the age steeped themselves in the classics, and admiration for figures of classical literature was a driving force in creating the era's political and social ideals. Lindley understood that he lacked the immersion in the classics that a university education would have provided, and which was obtained at King's College by later acquaintances such as Peter Van Shaack and John Jay. The French and English savants of the Enlightenment admired by Murray always stressed the importance of classical languages. So, soon after his return home to New York from Burlington, he persuaded his father to let him be tutored in the classics (as well as "liberal studies" and science).[30]

For Lindley, as for many Enlightenment figures, Latin was the more important of the languages. In his admiration for Latin authors (particularly Cicero, who appears often in his reading textbooks), he shared not only the taste of his age, but a commitment to virtuous conduct in public life. It is a theme repeated often in the *English Reader* and his other reading texts. Though he also believed an educated person should know Greek, it was mainly to be able to read the New Testament in that language.

For Lindley Murray, the classics were one part of the larger canvas of liberal education. Some years later, when it came time for another Lindley Murray, son of his brother John, to be educated, the great textbook writer laid out his theory of what an educated man should know. It is a blueprint for a liberal education (which includes science), and though written in the first decade of the nineteenth century, epitomizes late Enlightenment ideas on the subject.

From England, Lindley wrote to John Murray: ". . .perhaps thou would let him [young Lindley] be initiated in French, Latin and Greek, with some branches of the Mathematics, geography, History, Natural philosophy; and natural history, that is, Botany, mineralology, and animal nature. I should not be sorry to hear that, after a proper time, he inclined to study the elements of Hebrew." This formulation also retrospectively provides an insight into Lindley's mind in those early years when he sought to obtain the distinctions of "science and literature."[31]

Lindley also believed young women should acquire liberal education, or at least a "cultivated mind," though he believed that this education should be at a lower level of difficulty than for boys. "There are female duties, a character perfectly female, which are consistent with a good education, and a cultivated mind," he wrote to his niece, Alice Colden Willett. For her he recommended a selection of history, including Oliver Goldsmith's histories of Greece, Rome and England, William Robertson's histories of Charles V and of America, Elizabeth Hamilton's life of Agrippina and Middleton's life of Cicero.

In addition, Lindley advised his niece to read Guthrie's *Geographical Grammar*, Jedidiah Morse's *Geography and American Gazetteer*, the sermons of Hugh Blair, as well as volumes of poetry by Milton, James Thompson, Edward Young,

Mark Akenside and William Cowper. Several of these writers were included in Lindley's readers. In addition, though, Lindley recommended books specifically appropriate for females, such as Elizabeth Hamilton's *Letters on Education*, Gisbourne on the duties of the female sex and Doddridge's six-volume *Family Expositor*.[32] For his times, Lindley was enlightened about women, but he definitely saw their highest calling as raising a family. Two of his own female cousins were to go well beyond his limited vision. (See Chapter Eight).

The Enlightenment is a long historical process. In *The Enlightenment in America*, Henry May distinguishes four overlapping periods of Enlightenment thought in America, which span the era from 1688 through 1815. These are: (1) The Moderate Enlightenment (1688–1787), beginning with Newton and Locke, and preaching balance, order and religious compromise; (2) the Skeptical Enlightenment (1750–1789), whose "grand master is Voltaire," but also includes Hume; (3) the Revolutionary Enlightenment, which started with Rousseau and culminated with Thomas Paine and William Godwin; and (4) the Didactic Enlightenment (1800–1815), centered in Scotland, which believed in an "intelligible universe, clear and certain moral judgements and progress."[33]

This schema provides an insight into the style of Lindley Murray's Enlightenment education, which was almost entirely in the Moderate Enlightenment manner. *The Travels of Cyrus*, for example, used in the Quaker schools of Philadelphia in the 1750s, is an excellent specimen of the books that were being read, and the virtues extolled, early in the Enlightenment. All his life, Lindley Murray would show an extraordinary openness concerning the sources of religious and moral wisdom.

Lindley has less of a connection with the Skeptical Enlightenment, the second of Henry May's Enlightenment periods. Lindley's mind is certainly not a skeptical one. Indeed, he deals with this subject directly in the *Memoirs*, speaking of his youth:

My principles were never disturbed by infidelity or skepticism. I always had the happiness, since I was capable of reflecting on the subject, of having sentiments fixed in favor of the Christian religion; and no argument I ever met with, in company or in books, had any injurious effects upon me. Some of my acquaintance were either deists or skeptics; but I always found replies to their reasonings.[34]

Though no skeptic, Lindley was well aware, as is evident from the French-language reading texts he produced, of the opinions of Voltaire on literature. But his exclusion of Voltaire from the authors used in his French reading texts is significant. In excluding him, Lindley was defining his own intellectual position, drawing a line in the sand. He might use his ideas, but Voltaire's reputation as a radical caused Lindley concern.

In the years after he left America, Lindley would encounter the writers of the fourth of Henry May's Enlightenment periods, the Didactic, and certain writers of the Scottish Enlightenment who mainly created it. Among them he would find his final intellectual home, in a tradition that accepted the presuppositions of the Moderate Enlightenment, civic humanism and Christianity, though of an anti-Calvinist kind. It was those sentiments he enshrined in the reading texts he produced.

The Road to Revolution

5

$\mathbf{A}$S HE BEGAN HIS LEGAL PRACTICE in New York in 1767, Lindley was entering a different world. Boom times were over and the city had endured an economic depression. The fall of Quebec in 1759 presaged the end of the Seven Years' War in North America, though Montreal held out against British troops until late in 1760. With the end of the war, the customs value of imports plummeted from the pre-Revolution high of £483,952 in 1759 to £89,630 in 1761.[1] In addition to a slowing of transatlantic trade, communities throughout America had to face repayment of large war debts.

Robert Murray, child of the boom, was probably an early victim of the bust. The last advertisement for the firm of Murray and Pearsall in the *New York Gazette* appeared on September 15, 1760. By February 23, 1761, Pearsall was advertising on his own. From October 3, 1760, on, the Quaker merchant Joshua Delaplaine is found selling such items as fringe, silk hair and brown shalloon directly to Pearsall, rather than to the firm of Murray and Pearsall.[2]

In November 1765—the height of the depression—227 New York merchants petitioned the British House of Commons for relief from the ruin that a range of prohibitive duties was imposing on them. The British Government turned them down, causing a serious liquidity crisis and stagnating trade. As one New Yorker wrote in a letter: "Trade in this part of the world has come to so wretched a pass that you would imagine the plague has been here, the grass is growing in most trading streets, and the traders, so far from wanting the assistance of a clerk, rather want employment for themselves." "We have no butter to our bread," wrote another merchant to a friend in London in 1765.[3]

The passage of the Stamp Act in 1765 had made the depression worse. Anger at Britain over the proposed Stamp Act taxes also had political consequences, provoking the general populace. The Sons of Liberty group was organized to protest the act. For ten months beginning in July 1765, there was almost constant turmoil in New York City. On November 1, demonstrators burned the state coach owned by Lieut. Gov. Cadwallader Colden. On November 6, 1765, the Sons of Liberty passed a resolution declaring that no more goods coming from England should be sold on commission after January 1, 1766.[4] The unsettled political situation must have compounded Robert Murray's unease about his economic position.

Of course, Robert was not without his resources or his guile. As noted above, we see him in 1764 undercutting his competitors in the marine insurance business. This may have been a desperation measure, however. "In the postwar depression," notes one commentary, "a large number of newer fortunes were vulnerable to specie shortages, glutted markets for grain in the transatlantic markets, and competition from Philadelphia and New England."[5] The free-spending Robert Murray possessed one of these newer fortunes.

Robert also took other measures. When the early effects of the depression were setting in, he may have thought of moving his business to Philadelphia to take advantage of his alliances there. In 1763, he bought land in Philadelphia.[6] Finally, though, and perhaps spurred by the turmoil in New York, he decided to revive his fortunes by setting up in Britain. During 1765 or early 1766, at least a year before Lindley finished his legal studies, Robert went to London. As Lindley Murray describes it in the *Memoirs*, Robert traveled "on commercial matters of importance, which made his presence there, at that time, very expedient." After about a year, Robert was joined there by Lindley.[7]

Once Robert had established himself in London, he sent for his family, including his wife and his daughters Beulah and Susannah. The girls went to school in London and were even formally presented at court. And, a Murray descendant assures us, "as the Queen was partial to the Friends, they always received from her Majesty a gracious smile."[8]

Lindley was accompanied on his voyage by his new wife, the former Hannah Dobson, a Friend from Flushing, L.I. The couple had been married in 1767. Her father, Thomas Dobson, was a prominent member of the New York Yearly Meeting, later serving on the New York Meeting for Sufferings. Thomas Dobson's wife was Catherine Bowne, a member of a prominent Quaker family in Flushing, and a descendant of the famous seventeenth-century Quaker proselytizer John Bowne.

Hannah, Lindley testifies, was "a young woman of personal attractions, good sense, a most amiable disposition, and of a worthy and respectable family." The marriage of Lindley and Hannah had not been performed according to Friends' discipline, but on March 9, 1767, the Monthly Meeting held at Flushing accepted an apology from Lindley:

> After having seriously reflected upon the subject of my marriage I can with Truth and Sincerity say that I am very sorry to have acted in this Matter contrary to the Discipline of Friends, and without the Approbation of my parents: That I condemn it as being performed by a Priest; and upon the Whole I am sensibly concerned for every violation of the Good rules and order of your Society.—I therefore earnestly ask for the Continuance of your Care and Regard, which I will endeavour by my Future Conduct to merit and retain. Your respectful Frn:d Lindley Murray.

In the manuscript of the letter, in the phrase "I am very sorry" in the first sentence, one can clearly see that the words "I am" are written over the words "we are." Possibly, officials of the

Flushing Meeting were not willing to allow Lindley to implicate his bride in the decision to be married by a "priest."[9] According to Elizabeth Frank in the *Memoirs*, Hannah and Lindley celebrated June 22, 1809, as their forty-second anniversary. That would mean they remarried under Friends' discipline on June 22, 1767, and celebrated their marriage from that date.[10]

Robert Murray's new business was a partnership with fellow Quaker Philip Sansom of London. The firm was called Murray & Sansom, indicating, as was always the case with Robert, that he was the controlling partner. Robert's younger brother John handled the concern's business back in New York. Philip Sansom was undoubtedly linked to the prominent Quaker Sansom family of Philadelphia, who had close English connections.

Lindley Murray and his new bride, however, did not plan on living permanently in Britain. "It appeared probable," he says in the *Memoirs*, that in the course of a year, I should return to America." In the event, the couple stayed in Britain until late 1771. From the chronology, it seems that Lindley had gone to England to help his father with the explicit purpose of setting up the new business. Certainly, the assiduous Lindley did not just fritter away his time during these years, and it is more likely that he was involved in commercial than legal matters. It is a period Lindley does not discuss in depth in the *Memoirs*.[11]

Robert Murray, meanwhile, initially returned to New York in 1768. With Lindley apparently representing the family's interests in England, Robert resumed his business activities, and became a founding member of the New York Chamber of Commerce on April 5, 1768.[12] Two weeks later, on April 18, the following news item appeared in the *New York Mercury*:

> A very beneficial Branch of Trade has long been neglected in this Province, that is, Whaling; but we now have some Hopes of seeing it revived, as Mr. Robert Murray, and Messrs. Franklin have at their own Expense, fitted out a Sloop for that Purpose, which sailed yesterday.

There is no evidence whether this venture succeeded, but New York never did become a major whaling port.

Robert resumed his Quaker activities as well, joining the members of the New York Meeting for Sufferings. However, after August 1, 1769, Robert stopped attending meetings of the Chamber and returned to London. On September 1, 1772, the Chamber secretary made a rare notation of where absent members were located, and placed Robert in London.[13] He was apparently back in New York once again by 1773 when he declined an invitation to serve on the Meeting for Sufferings.[14]

Once he returned to New York in 1771, Lindley also resumed his previous interests. He became one of the 140 subscribers who formed the Union Library Society's library with nearly 1,000 volumes, and one of its twelve directors. Quakers were represented in this enterprise—other directors included Walter Franklin and Robert Bowne (now a relation of Lindley through his wife Hannah), who was treasurer. Unfortunately, the society's books were destroyed or scattered during the British occupation of New York and the great fire of 1776.[15]

As events gathered speed toward the approaching Revolution, Lindley began to represent the family on important New York bodies, which were charged with enforcing on colonial merchants the non-importation agreements that had grown up in the wake of the Townshend Acts and other measures. Gradually, these committees became the most important political entities in the city.

During Robert's absence in Britain, his affairs in New York had been conducted by his younger brother John. John was born in 1741 and was two decades younger than Robert, and while his brother lived, he was always in his shadow.

John's rise in Robert's businesses was gradual. At this point, Robert had two separate firms. One was Murray & Sansom, the international trading business. In 1771, the firm's name was changed to Murray, Sansom & Co., apparently reflecting John

Murray's rise to at least a junior partnership. After Robert's death in 1786, John became the chief American partner in Murray & Sansom, and the firm continued into the nineteenth century.

Robert's other business was Robert Murray & Co., which handled mainly domestic investments, including several stores in the New York area. One in Elizabethtown, New Jersey, was operated by Ichabod Barnet, who was married to Robert's eldest daughter, Mary. John Murray also became a junior partner in this second business. His growing role in it was reflected in a name change after the Revolution to "Robert and John Murray." After Robert's death, it evolved into John Murray & Co.

Though John Murray had remained a Presbyterian, and his political sentiments apparently differed from Robert's, the Murrays were always a close-knit clan, and while Robert lived, John's actions in business matters were subordinated to, or coordinated with, Robert's wishes.

Robert Murray played some public role in Quaker affairs as a member for several years of the New York Meeting for Sufferings, but he normally used John Murray as a front man for the family in civic bodies. John was a member of the Committee of 51, organized in New York in May 1774 to deal with matters relating to British commercial legislation. It was controlled by the more conservative of the city's merchants. But Parliament's passage in 1774 of what the colonists termed the Intolerable Acts (passed in response to the Boston Tea Party) roused an anti-British fervor in the colonies and led to the First Continental Congress (September 5–October 26), which forbade importation and use of British goods.

Responding to the acts of the Congress and resolved to enforce nonimportation, the Committee of 60 was formed in New York City in November 1774, succeeding the Committee of 51. John Murray was not a member of the new group; the family was represented by Lindley Murray.

However, the new nonimportation militancy caused concern in Quaker circles of the time. As Hugh Barbour and J. William

Frost put it in *The Quakers*, "Friends feared that the momentum of the committees and the protest might lead to violence and the undermining of legitimate authority."[16]

The issue of militancy was a watershed for America's Quakers. Friends' reservations about the growing threat of war that nonimportation portended caused them to expel some members while others left the Society of Friends voluntarily. Ultimately, the Quakers' position led to criticism from patriots that they had supported the Crown in the Revolution. Evidence on the anguish that this period brought to the Society of Friends' community emerges from the records of the Meetings for Sufferings.

In Philadelphia, where divisions on a similar nonimportation committee had led to violent confrontations, the Meeting for Sufferings took the lead in formulating the Quaker case. In November 1774, Philadelphia wrote to the New York Friends, expressing "a brotherly concern for steady watchfulness for maintaining our peaceable Testimony in these times of peril" and urging that "such friends as are on publick Committees" be dissuaded from serving.

The matter was first noted on December 7, 1774, in the minutes of the New York Meeting for Sufferings. Like its Philadelphia counterpart, this served as a kind of executive committee of the full New York Meeting. (One of the New York Meeting for Sufferings' most prominent members was Thomas Dobson, Lindley's father-in-law; he had intermittently been a member of the group since as early as 1758 and had become a member again on June 1, 1773.)[17] The New York Meeting for Sufferings notes an epistle received from Philadelphia expressing "a brotherly concern for a steady watchfulness for maintaining our peaceable testimony in these times of peril."

"Some among us," the New York minutes state, "have been appointed on a committee for enforcing certain resolves entered into on principles repugnant to our profession." This committee consisted of John Burling, Henry Haydock and Tideman Hull.

The trio urged Quaker members to resign from the Committee of 60 and were successful in several instances. But two Friends, Lindley Murray and Lancaster Burling, defied the pressures and continued to serve.[18]

The topic of "the Friends who are on publick committees" continued to be the main, or at least an important part, of every agenda of the New York Meeting for Sufferings for several months. After the Battles of Lexington and Concord in April, the Committee of 60 was quickly expanded and became the Committee of 100. On May 25, the Minutes of the New York Meeting for Sufferings report that "no further progress" had been made in persuading Murray and Burling to resign. Indeed, "a further deviation from our Christian testimony was of late apparant." The matter was considered so serious that it was decided "to lay the same before the ensuing yearly meeting." This is the last time the question of those serving on the "publick committees" specifically comes up in the minutes of the Meeting for Sufferings.

A similar issue arose again two years later, in the minutes of the Meeting for Sufferings of May 23, 1777, after the British had occupied New York City. It was reported that Governor Tryon had met with some Friends and told them that "a number of our society had incurred the displeasure of the Government by being too busy and too active in the present commotions." Tryon used this fact to attempt to twist the arms of the Quakers to provide stockings, mittens or other assistance for troops loyal to the Crown.[19] The Quakers did not yield to Tryon's prodding, but it is interesting to speculate about who was "too busy and too active." The most likely suspect is not Lindley Murray, but rather Lancaster Burling, who had fully embraced the patriot cause and was operating as a privateer against British shipping. Burling had been expelled from the Society the year before for his activities.

As the New York Meeting for Sufferings continued to press Burling and Lindley Murray to resign from "publick committees" in the early months of 1775, something was brewing that would have serious consequences for Lindley's future—the *Beulah* affair.

2

THE SUCCESS (OR FAILURE) OF THE NEW YORK nonimportation committee hinged on its ability to block the unloading of ships coming from Britain. The key date was February 1, 1775. Article 10 of the Continental Association—the nonimportation organization subscribed to by all the colonies—decreed that after February 1, any goods should be sent back "forthwith" and "without breaking any of the packages thereof."[20]

The first vessel arriving in the port of New York after February 1 was the *James*, which docked at Robert Murray's wharf in New York with a load of coal and dry goods. An angry crowd soon gathered, and its captain moved the *James* into the bay for safety. But the captain brought the *James* back into town on February 9 under the protection of a British naval vessel. Soon after he debarked, the captain was seized by the nonimportation camp and scornfully paraded through the city. Two days later, the *James* fled New York.

The British Navy, not wanting to admit defeat at the hands of the patriots, demanded that the ship's owners give formal acquiescence to such a departure by obtaining clearance for it from the New York Custom House. One of the owners, a Mr. Buchanan, quickly made the arrangements.

"Buchanan's prudent conduct," says one commentator, "was in dramatic contrast to that of Robert and John Murray."[21] For the next ship that tried to break the blockade belonged to Robert Murray and his firm of Murray & Sansom, in which John Murray also worked. The *Beulah's* attempt to land goods surreptitiously, made worse by an attempted cover-up instigated by the Murrays, caused deep embarrassment and consternation for the family. It gave the Murrays a wide reputation for opposing the patriot cause and almost resulted in the expulsion of Robert and John Murray from New York City. It was also likely an important factor in the exile of Lindley Murray from New York a decade later.

The ship *Beulah*, named after Robert's second daughter, arrived off New York from Britain on February 17, but was blocked from entering the harbor by a patrol boat of the committee of inspection led by the zealous Isaac Sears, "with other virtuous citizens."[22] On February 20, the Murrays petitioned the New York committee for an exemption to allow the *Beulah* to land, arguing that the goods had been ordered before the non-importation strictures had been agreed to. The argument was rejected. The *Beulah* would likely have left Britain in December. News of the actions of the Continental Congress would certainly have been known in Britain by then, so the voyage had been undertaken with the likelihood that it would face entry problems.

The Committee of 60 ordered the ship out of the port. After lying in the Narrows for three weeks amid storms and high seas, under the watchful eye of the committee, the *Beulah* on March 5 moved to Sandy Hook on the edge of New York Bay, ostensibly to await a favorable wind for the return voyage to England. A squall forced the committee's patrol boat, which did not have as deep a keel as the *Beulah*, to find haven. This was the chance the Murrays were waiting for. They had previously arranged for a boat from Elizabethtown, New Jersey, to be waiting for the *Beulah* off Staten Island under cover of darkness.

The vessel that did the unloading had been hired by one Samuel Lee of Elizabeth, a boatman. Lee was employed for the job by Ichabod Barnet, Robert Murray's son-in-law and manager of the Murray store in Elizabeth. For the unloading of the *Beulah*, Lee was accompanied by John Murray himself; Barnet; John Graham, who was a clerk and partner with John Murray in his New York store; and Samuel Reed, a nephew of Robert and John who also worked for them.

It must have been a hard night's work. The Murray party, presumably aided by the crew of the *Beulah*, transferred between a ton and a half and two tons of goods, including 84 bolts of Russia duck (sail cloth), numerous bolts of other fabric and five bales of pepper. The goods were moved to Barnet's store in Elizabeth. Sears found out about it and alerted the Elizabeth non-importation committee, which called in Lee and Barnet for questioning.

The Elizabeth committee members initially reported to New York in a message dated March 11. According to their account, Lee and Barnet had tried to stonewall and deceive the committee. Lee, the Elizabeth committee said, "cannot be persuaded to give any clear information on the matter, he being under the apprehension that he by that means may be the ruin of some particular persons in New York." Barnet boldly "refused to answer the questions proposed to him," but offered to swear—a bald-faced lie—"that no goods from the *Beulah* were landed in the town [Elizabeth]." This statement, the Elizabeth committee reported, "we did not accept."[23]

As so often happens, this cover-up seemed to spur the anger of the Elizabeth committee; in the temper of the time, that undoubtedly meant threats against the Barnet family. One reason for the strong feelings was that the Murrays' attempt to break the importation ban could (and in the event did) cause serious damage to New York's reputation with other colonial committees. The issue had grave implications for colonial unity, particularly because the Murrays were so commercially prominent, and because John Murray had been one of the merchants who voted to break a previous nonimportation agreement in 1770.

The Elizabeth committee pressed the case, and Samuel Lee soon confessed. In a deposition dated March 13, he said he had been hired by Barnet, had done the unloading with the help of Barnet, John Murray and John Graham, and had deposited the goods at Barnet's store in Elizabeth. With Lee's confession, the Murrays' attempted cover-up was exposed. So John Murray appeared before the New York committee the same day to confess. He made a deposition, dated March 15, giving a full account of what happened. On the same date, Robert Murray submitted a short deposition affirming the facts in John Murray's statement.

In a letter the same day to the Elizabeth committee, the Murrays declared their readiness to reship the goods unloaded from the *Beulah*, adding that they regretted the "imprudent measure" and the "trouble and uneasiness it has given to our fellow citizens." As penance, they pledged £200 towards repairing a hospital in Elizabeth that had recently been destroyed by fire.

This measure apparently satisfied the Elizabeth committee, but there was still the New York committee to deal with. The question of the Murrays' punishment was an item of business for the Committee of 60 for several weeks. We know this because Alexander McDougall, a leader of the "Friends of Liberty" and a committee member whom George Washington later called one of the "pillars of the Revolution," kept notes on the back of the notices for each meeting. These notes are housed at the New-York Historical Society.[24]

On March 15, McDougall records, the committee appointed merchant Francis Lewis to head a subcommittee to make recommendations following the John Murray confession, while at the same time appointing John Jay to prepare a letter to surrounding counties to mend fences in the wake of the *Beulah* affair.

At a special meeting the next day, it was agreed that a full account of the *Beulah* affair should be inserted in the next issue of "Holt's paper" (the *New York Journal*). The account, reprinting in full the various depositions, covers nearly four long columns in the issue of Thursday, March 23. The *Journal* account lists Lindley Murray as being one of the members of the Committee of 60 in attendance on March 16.

However, the agreement to publish the sordid details did not end the business. At the committee of March 20, according to McDougall's scribbled notes, it "was argued what should be considered satisfactory from Messrs. Murray." The committee chair, Isaac Low, maintained "that in his opinion they had given full Satisfaction, & that the association required no more, the penalty intended was the Publishing the name of the offender." McDougall says he "disputed with him," obviously arguing for a stiffer penalty.[25]

There is no question that the Murrays' attempt to break the ban with the *Beulah* coalesced public opinion against them. Opposition rose immediately. "The People," Peter R. Livingston had written to a friend on February 19 about the *Beulah*, "are determined that she shall go back."[26] After the Murrays' confession, some among the outraged public were urging a boycott of the Murrays' stores, but McDougall and Isaac Sears wanted more severe punishment. As reported in the *New York Journal*, they and their followers felt that an example should be made and the Murrays banished from the city.[27] Though it is not recorded in his notes, McDougall apparently raised this threat at the March 20 meeting.

In a letter dated March 20, possibly written in the wake of the committee meeting, the dire prospect of exile caused Mary Lindley Murray to plead for leniency for her husband Robert and brother-in-law John. She wrote McDougall and Sears, begging their "Intercession to prevent an Evil, which if brought upon them, must involve their innocent Wives and helpless children in Unspeakable Distress." The lawyer and historian William Smith, a sometime counselor to the Sons of Liberty, urged McDougall to respond to Mrs. Murray in "the tenderest Terms."[28]

This impassioned letter, perhaps bolstered by Mary Lindley Murray's reputation as someone sympathetic to the Whig cause, worked.[29] Banishment was averted. But there seems to have been a financial penalty for the Murrays. At the meeting of March 27, according to McDougall, Sears brought in an account of expenses incurred by the committee's patrol boat, "& proposed, subscriptions being opened" in the committee and the town for payment. Even supporters of the Murrays seem to have balked at chipping in to defray the boat's expenses. This led to a compromise, with the Murrays picking up the patrol boat costs, because at the meeting of April 1, "It was unanimously determined that Messrs. Murray, might according to the Association pay their Debts" in bills of exchange.[30]

Of even greater importance to the Committee than punishment of the Murrays was the repair of the damage to New York's reputation among other colonies. Indeed, McDougall feared the Murrays' action would have "a fatal consequence on the Councils of the Nation."[31] Although some Quakers had refused to deal with the committees of inspection as a matter of principle, Robert Murray was not motivated by anything but commercial advantage,[32] and everyone knew it.

The Committee of 60 was forced to go out of its way to assuage the fears of other nonimportation committees concerning the Murrays' attempt. As news of the affair had spread, the Committee of 60 received a communication from the New Haven committee dated March 6, enclosing an anonymous letter that spoke of the "weakness of the friends of Liberty." On behalf of the Committee of 60, John Jay wrote a mollifying letter to New Haven, assuring the committee that "the People in general are zealous in the Cause."[33]

The prevention of the *James* and *Beulah* from landing their goods was in fact a significant victory for the cause of nonimportation, and its enemies realized it. "The success which the violent party have had in preventing their vessels from landing their cargoes has given them great spirits," wrote Lieut. Gov. Cadwallader Colden, an ally of the Murrays, to Lord Dartmouth in Britain. "Your Lordships will believe it has chagrined me a good deal."[34]

On April 19, the battles of Lexington and Concord—in effect a colonial declaration of war—changed the situation completely. Within a few days, the Committee of 60 had been transformed into the more radical Committee of 100. Lindley Murray initially continued membership in that committee. But soon after, amid the fallout from the *Beulah* affair and subject to continuing pressure from his Quaker brethren, he went into exile with his wife at Islip, Long Island, near Great South Bay, 40 miles from New York, where he would remain until 1779.[35] It was an exile that would be repeated on a more significant scale nine years later.

What had been Lindley Murray's political position on the Committee of 60 during the *Beulah* Affair? A spectrum of political positions was being espoused in the deliberations of the Committee of 60 and in the Committee of 100. There is no evidence from the Quaker stand, which was one of principle, or from the deliberations of the committees themselves, to hint at which positions Lindley Murray was advocating. Twenty-two members of the Committee of 60, including Lindley, eventually became loyalists.[36]

On the one hand, it could be argued that Lindley was probably lining up with the more conservative elements on the committee. After all, Robert and Lindley Murray ultimately ended up in the loyalist camp; normally there is a consistent and logical trajectory towards such an outcome. There is also the evidence from Lindley Murray's *Memoirs*, which are striking in their avoidance of the least discussion of Lindley's public service. Since the *Memoirs* are meant to be exculpatory, Lindley would be expected to include anything that strengthened his case in the United States, but he never mentions his service on the Committee of 60.

On the other hand, there can be no doubt that Lindley was completely Whiggish in his philosophy, which normally would have made him sympathetic to the patriotic cause. There are numerous instances, however, of Whigs who remained loyal to the crown.[37] In addition, in the face of Quaker pressure, Lindley continued to serve on the Committee of 60 and on the Committee of 100. Decades later, as he grew into old age, Lindley's questions to his brother John about old friends from the Committee of 60 more often concern those who ended up on the patriotic side, such as his mentor Benjamin Kissam and his much admired fellow member of the Debating Club, John Jay, than of those who became loyalists. But considering the enmity roused by the *Beulah* affair, it is impossible to conceive that Lindley Murray was lining up on the Committee of 60 with opponents of his family.

A third possibility—one that I think comes closest to the truth—is that Lindley stayed politically neutral on the committees, but simply concentrated on defending his family's commercial interests. At the very moment when Lindley was resisting pressure by the New York Meeting to resign from the Committee of 60, for example, Robert Murray was preparing the *Beulah*'s transport of goods from Britain to New York, an enterprise of which Lindley must have been well aware. Lindley's presence on the committee was an aid to Robert's plans. The deep resentment that led to Lindley's expulsion from the country was, I believe, directly linked more to the great harm caused to New York's reputation by the *Beulah* affair than by any other particular actions. By all rights, it was Robert who should have been forced to leave America, but Lindley bore the brunt of public anger over his father's imprudence.

Lindley's loyalty to his family's commercial ventures was his most important consideration. But when he eventually abandoned service on the Committee of 100, pressure by fellow Quakers no doubt played some role in that decision. He and his wife left for Islip, Long Island, during 1775, around the time that the Meeting for Sufferings had recommended his membership on the Committee of 100 be brought before the yearly meeting. Lindley certainly did not want to be expelled from the Society of Friends. He had done his duty for his family on the Committees of 60 and 100, but political neutrality on the Committee of 100 was becoming more difficult, and continued refusal to resign posed a danger to the family's wide network of Quaker business contacts. There was also the possibility, as we shall see, of profitable business on Long Island.

But, as Lindley describes it in the *Memoirs*, there was another dimension. "We concluded to remain," he says of the move to Islip, "till the political storm should blow over."[38] In Lindley's view, the nonimportation controversy was just another bit of hubbub caused by agitators such as Alexander McDougall, Isaac Sears and John Lamb. Lindley Murray did not comprehend, as so many others did, what was happening in the colonies and what would be the eventual result. He thought of it as another "political storm." That was a serious miscalculation. Robert and John Murray, on the other hand, were more shrewd.

3

THE *BEULAH* AFFAIR WAS WIDELY REPORTED in newspapers along the eastern seaboard. Word of it reached Joseph Hoff, manager of the Hibernia iron works in Morris County, New Jersey, in which the Murrays held a controlling interest. In a letter of March 15, 1775, he asked the Murrays for more information on the incident, concerned that goods that had been promised to the iron works might have been lost: "I was much alarmed this day by a Rumour prevailing here that the Cargo of the Ship Bulia [sic] was burnt by the Committee on their order on Staten Island, if you have time I could wish to hear some Circumstances of the matter that I might contradict what may be said to yr. prejudice in this Quarter."[39] The misspelling of the ship's name indicates that the intelligent Hoff received news of the incident by word of mouth, and his remarks clearly show that the incident could be expected to cause ill feeling against the Murrays.

The Murrays' involvement in the iron business had begun in 1774, when they purchased an interest in the Hibernia Furnace, a rich mine of magnetite iron ore and a smelter in the hills of northern Morris County, New Jersey, in the heart of Jersey's iron country.[40] The purchase was made from William Alexander, undoubtedly well-known to the Murrays as a partner in the New York merchant firm of Livingston & Alexander.

Alexander had laid claim to the Earlship of Stirling in Scotland. The claim was refused by Parliament, but was widely recognized in the colonies, and he styled himself Lord Stirling. Stirling, who had built a mansion in Basking Ridge, New Jersey, in 1761, had bought a partial interest in the furnace in 1768 and was likely the sole owner by 1771, devoting himself wholly to the furnace.[41] The free-spending Stirling was deeply in debt, and the

Hibernia works were not profitable, at least until hostilities began in 1775. (In the long run, the mine was immensely profitable. From 1807 through 1907, it produced 5 million tons of ore.)[42]

In 1774, Stirling offered the whole yearly output of the furnace to any New York merchant who would supply the equipment and store goods needed to continue operations, but apparently had no takers.[43] He made a similar offer again the following year, offering to provide the annual production of the furnace to any merchant who would supply him with about £4,500 of goods for the use of the mine and its workers. Doubtless sensing how important iron would be in any coming hostilities, Robert and John Murray, through the firm of Murray & Sansom, took Stirling up on his offer; the Murrays seem to have become full owners, although some provision was likely made for Stirling's participation in any profits.[44]

It was a sagacious investment for the Murrays. In addition to understanding the importance of iron in a war, they had ships that could carry exports of pig iron to Britain. The export of iron ore to Britain had gradually increased since the days of the Durham Furnace. By 1771, the colonies were sending off more than 5,000 tons annually.[45]

The Murrays brought financial stability to an operation that had been losing money. Prodded constantly by their efficient mine manager Joseph Hoff, they saw to it that the operation had enough equipment and that the company store was properly stocked. Most of the goods for the works, including powder for blasting, were provided by the Murrays through Robert's son-in-law, the merchant Ichabod Barnet in Elizabeth.[46]

Once supplied with the necessary equipment (particularly powder) and goods for its laborers, the Hibernia Furnace turned out a steady flow of iron. The Murrays had previously been customers (or partial owners) of the furnace before taking major control. They had taken delivery of 44 tons of pig iron from the 1774 blast out of a total of 551 produced. From the spring blast in 1775, they took 120 tons. In his letter confirming the 1775 shipment, Hoff adds that "the powder that came from philadelphia is much damaged"—showing that the Murrays had involved some of their merchant contacts in Philadelphia in servicing the operation.[47]

As the year 1775 wore on, New York agitation against the British by such groups as the Sons of Liberty grew, particularly after the battles of Lexington and Concord in April. The Murrays apparently suffered at the hands of the agitators. Hoff writes on August 31: "I am very sorry to hear of the disturbance in yr. place, to the Concern you must have been in on that Occasion."

As the conflict between the Americans and British became more intense, the furnace was of course looked to as a potential source of ordnance. On April 6, 1775, two weeks before the battles of Lexington and Concord, Hoff writes to the Murrays that a Henry Wissner, Esq., of Goshen, New York, has inquired about buying a large cannon. Two days later, Hoff tells the Murrays that Lord Stirling has informed him that "if we can get moulders he will find us work making cannon." On June 9, Hoff writes his employers that he has produced a prototype.

But in July 1776, a large British invasion force aimed at New York arrived in Staten Island.[48] The potential hostilities must have caused much alarm among New Yorkers, and the merchant class must have wondered about the fate of its businesses. It drove the Murrays, as subsequent events show, into a panic. On August 20, 1776, Hoff writes to Robert Murray, saying he is addressing the correspondence to him "on acct. of Mr. John Murray's absence." On September 11, Hoff writes to Robert: "I do not understand what you mean by desireing me to apply to Mr. Jn. Murray at Phila it is upwards of 100 miles from here."

What had happened was that John Murray had left New York and gone to the City of Brotherly Love. By instructing Hoff to refer to John for decisions, Robert was of course lessening the likelihood of a paper trail linking him to manufacture of arms for the patriot cause. The rather hurt and astonished response of the hard-working Hoff to Robert Murray's letter gives an inkling of the peremptoriness of Robert's missive.

A letter of Lindley Murray of 1793 likely refers to John Murray's trip at this time: "I remember that, during the War, Uncle went to Philadelphia to secure a flour contract for the benefit of M S [Murray Sansom & Co.]; I think that previous to his embarking, lest he might never return, he settled his outward affairs as well as he could." If this was the same trip, the "flour contract" was at least in part a cover story that Robert and John made up.[49]

From the timing of John Murray's journey, just before the British move against Brooklyn, it is evident that the Murrays had concluded they must act to protect the family business. They were placing bets on each side in the conflict. If the British were victorious in the coming battle for the city, Robert would maintain the base in New York and deal with them; John, headquartered for the moment in Philadelphia, would be in a position to deal with the patriots and the Hibernia mine.

This strategy led to the establishment of yet another Murray enterprise. After John Murray arrived in Philadelphia some time before August 20, he quickly put together a partnership to use Hibernia's output to manufacture and sell sheet metal. The partnership was called Murray, Griffiths and Bullard. In the *Pennsylvania Evening Post* on September 12, the new firm ran an advertisement for such items as camp kettles and frying pans.

But events in New York were taking a turn that put the wisdom of the Murrays' strategy in question. The British under Gen. Sir William Howe had soundly whipped George Washington's patriot army in the Battle of Brooklyn at the end of August. On September 15, Howe's troops invaded Manhattan and caused the patriot force to flee their positions in the south of the island. Over the next weeks, the British consolidated their control of the city and its immediate surroundings.

Observing these developments, the Murrays apparently decided to give the British most—though not all—of their allegiance. We can discern the shift from another advertisement in the *Pennsylvania Evening Post* that appeared April 24, 1777. In it,

John Bullard, the third member of the Murray partnership, offers iron and copper items for sale to clients including "gentlemen of the American army." But the ad also states that the partnership of Murray, Griffiths and Bullard formed on September 12, 1776, had been dissolved after less than a month, on October 5, 1776.[50] By that date, Robert Murray had obviously decided to cast the family's lot with the Crown. His brother's open enterprise supplying the patriot army could not continue.

Before he could return to New York from Philadelphia, however, John Murray had to settle the future of the Hibernia mine. Joseph Hoff's letters reveal he traveled to Philadelphia in September to meet John, but was unable to see him, an indication of John's feverish work on the new partnership.[51] Then, on November 14, Hoff wrote to Lord Stirling that John had made an inspection tour of Hibernia:

> Mr. John Murray has been upp to see the Works and appeard much pleas'd with every transaction here, but informs me that as the Connection between him and his brother Robert Murray is cut off, at present he is not Capacitated to supply me with Money to lay in a Stock of provisions—employ men & for the ensueing Blast but has directed me to apply for the amount of the Shott now makeing for the public use and to appropriate the Money to the above purpose—(We have already completed Shott to the amout. of £1000 and makeing daily and exceding good & neat, I have wrote Coll Knox (a copy of which I enclose) to represent the matter properly to the Genl. and now to send me by my brother Charles £1000. I must take the liberty to ask yr. Lordships assistance in the matter if necessary.

John's instructions to Hoff seem clear. He was to seek business for ammunition from the Continental army and to use Stirling as a go-between. The role of Stirling, now a general in the Continental army, hero of the Battle of Brooklyn, and still possibly a minority partner in the Hibernia enterprise, was to use his influence to help obtain orders and payment. (Even outside of his military role, Stirling was not new to military procurement politicking. During the Seven Years' War, his New York firm of Livingston and Alexander had obtained a contract to supply the provincial troops in the attack on Niagara.)[52]

The Hibernia Furnace made cannon balls and grapeshot for the Continental Army for the remainder of the Revolution. In 1777, Charles Hoff, who took over the forge after the death of his brother Joseph, wrote to Gov. Livingston of New Jersey: "We made last year for the Publick Service upwards of 120 tons of shott."[53] So while the Murrays were making money from trade with the British in New York, they were also profiting from the patriot side.

Once again, though, the Murrays may have been taking the proceeds in iron, which may well have been going to John Bullard in Philadelphia, who continued to turn out iron as well as copper products for potential use by the Continental Army.

Having at least officially cut his ties with the Philadelphia partnership, and given Hoff his marching orders, John Murray was able to return to New York to participate in the wealth of commercial possibilities that had opened up there.

It is interesting to consider the nature of John Murray's own political sentiments. John was never listed as a loyalist by the historian Lorenzo Sabine in his 1864 book on the subject. Though he had a Quaker wife, John had remained a Presbyterian, which normally might have made him sympathetic to the patriot cause. In his visit to Joseph Hoff, John emphasized his break with Robert Murray. But Hoff, as the evidence shows, was continually kept in the dark about the Murrays' real plans. A clearer hint about John Murray's actions is given by Lindley Murray's 1793 letter about John's trip to Philadelphia. In Lindley's estimation, John was simply carrying on the family business.

This seems the most sensible construction to put on the Murrays' machinations. Though he no doubt chaffed at times under his brother's direction, John Murray was always a loyal right hand to Robert. Both brothers saw family solidarity as the key to survival amid the storms of the time. At the same time, the work of the Hibernia mine for the patriots may well have become a mitigating factor for John Murray in the postwar era when the fate of those who traded with the British was being weighed.

The Revolution and Its Aftermath

6

R OBERT MURRAY'S ANALYSIS of the
military situation in New York soon proved correct. The British
made short work of George Washington's troops in the Battle of
Brooklyn in late August 1776. But Lord Stirling, the Murrays'
associate in the Hibernia Mine, emerged as a hero, leading continual charges against a British stronghold that enabled other
patriot troops to escape to safety. "General Lord Stirling fought
like a wolf," Lord Cornwallis said later. Stirling's bravery certainly did not diminish the prospects of the Hibernia mine for
obtaining work from the Continental Army.

In the Battle of Manhattan in September 1776, which followed soon after the Brooklyn defeat, the Murray family was
involved in an incident that later gained much notoriety, and
evolved into an enduring bit of New York folklore. Upon arriving
in Manhattan, the British General Sir William Howe loitered in
the agreeable precincts of Inclenberg while awaiting the arrival of
regiments from across the East River. It was not unusual for visitors of high standing to make such stops—Gen. George
Washington had made Inclenberg his headquarters for a day a
short while before, on September 14.[1]

The Washington visit faded from history, but not Howe's.
According to a legend that later sprung up, Mary Lindley Murray
and her charming daughters—particularly Beulah and
Susannah—consciously kept Howe and his officers entertained

66

and distracted, enabling George Washington's troops (under General Israel Putnam) to escape northward, thus saving the Continental Army to fight another day.[2]

The legend is commemorated in a plaque at Park Avenue and Thirty-Seventh Street in New York City, which reads:

IN HONOR OF
MARY LINDLEY MURRAY
FOR SERVICES RENDERED HER COUNTRY
DURING THE AMERICAN REVOLUTION, ENTERTAINING
AT HER HOME, ON THIS SITE,
GEN. HOWE AND HIS OFFICERS, UNTIL THE
AMERICAN TROOPS UNDER GEN. PUTNAM ESCAPED.
SEPTEMBER 15, 1776   NOVEMBER 25, 1903
ERECTED BY
KNICKERBOCKER CHAPTER, NEW YORK
DAUGHTERS OF THE AMERICAN REVOLUTION

The incident was also the subject of two Broadway plays. One was *Dearest Enemy* (1925), the first Broadway hit of Rodgers and Hart. Robert Sherwood took up the theme again three decades later in *A Small War in Murray Hill*, which was produced posthumously in 1957.[3]

Serious historians, however, are unanimous in feeling the incident at Murray Hill is overblown, and that Howe would not personally have moved until all his troops, cavalry and artillery had landed. Howe's cautious, orthodox battle plan called for the establishment of a secure beachhead on Manhattan before proceeding. He had already done everything called for in his plan for the day. The collapse of resistance among Gen. Israel Putnam's troops in the southern part of the island (and their subsequent scramble northward under the cover of forest) did not change his agenda.[4]

But like most legends, the story of Mary Lindley Murray and General Howe does seem to have a nub of truth in it. The tale was not contrived later—the earliest source dates to immediately after the incident. James Thacher, M.D., a gossipy surgeon with the Continental Army, kept a journal that is one of the prime sources of information about the military happenings of the times. In an entry for September 20, Thacher tells the story as follows:

> The British generals... repaired to the house of a Mr. Robert Murray, a Quaker and friend of our cause; Mrs. Murray treated them with cake and wine, and they were induced to tarry two hours or more, Governor Tryon frequently joking her about her American friends. By this happy incident general Putnam, by continuing his march, escaped... It has since become almost a common saying among our officers, that Mrs. Murray saved this part of the American army."[5]

Thacher is of course wrong about Robert Murray's allegiance, but the description of Mary Lindley Murray as pro-patriot does ring true. Remember that Mary's father had been an anti-establishment politician in Pennsylvania. Indeed, some members of the Lindley family served the Revolutionary cause. Jonathan Lindley, a resident of North Carolina and grandson of Mary's uncle, James Lindley, Jr., served as a Revolutionary soldier. Jonathan's brother, Thomas, was also a patriot. The Battle of Lindley's Mill was fought in North Carolina on his property on September 14, 1781. (John Lindley, yet another brother of the same family, was however a Tory; his story is told below.)[6]

In addition, two sons of Mary Lindley Murray's aunt Isabella (who had married Robert's uncle William) also served in the Revolutionary Army. James Murray (b. 1729) was a captain and John Murray (b. 1731) commanded a rifle company with Washington's forces and in fact had participated in the Battle of Brooklyn, which immediately preceded Howe's invasion of Manhattan. Yet another cousin of the family, Robert Dixon, had fallen in the Battle of Brooklyn. He has been described as "the first Pennsylvania offering to the cause of Independence."

Pennsylvanians had borne much of the brunt of the battle and had suffered numerous casualties.[7]

Though a proper and loyal wife, Mary probably differed politically from her husband, feeling sympathy for the patriots' cause. Indeed, some sources describe her as a "warm Whig." This tendency might well be the nub of truth in the tale of Mary Lindley Murray and General Howe in the small war on Murray Hill. The tale later became entwined with charges, especially from embittered loyalists, that General Howe and his brother, Admiral Lord Richard Howe, had not vigorously pursued the war in America, especially after the defeat of Washington in the Battle of Brooklyn.

Whatever the true story is, it seems it did not prevent Murray Hill from becoming a gathering place for the British during the occupation of New York. According to one nineteenth-century account, Inclenberg at this period "was crowded with scarlet coats and powdered wigs."[8]

2

BEFORE THE BATTLE OF BROOKLYN, on Long Island, Lindley and Robert Murray, in the grand tradition of the Murray family, investigated yet another way of making money. They were having a fling at the business of making salt.

In the colonial oceanside settlements, fishing was an important industry. Inland, the fur trade remained a vibrant facet of colonial commerce. For the general populace, preserved meat was an established part of their diet. What these enterprises had in common was that they required large amounts of salt. It was a key element in the preserving of fish and meat and in the curing of skins. The largest supplier of salt for the colonists had been Salt Tortuga in the Leeward Islands, but the product was also brought in from the Azores and the Canary Islands. In addition, the Middle Atlantic colonies imported salt from neighbors, including Massachusetts and Virginia.[9]

But as soon as the Revolution started, this commerce was interrupted, and there was an immediate shortage of salt, which was made worse by a British naval blockade. As a result, as Lindley Murray reports in his *Memoirs*, the Continental Congress "found it necessary to recommend and encourage the making" of salt. Congress first took action on December 19, 1775, when it "earnestly recommended to the several Assemblies and Conventions to promote by sufficient public encouragement the making of salt in their respective Colonies." By May 1776, the situation had grown more desperate and Congress established a bounty "of a dollar p'r bushel" (a bushel weighed 55 pounds) for all "salt as shall be imported into or manufactured" over the next year.[10]

There is nothing like a government subsidy to quicken the entrepreneurial heart, but an additional incentive was sharply rising prices for salt. Before the advent of war, salt could have been had for about 20 to 25 pence a bushel. By 1777, salt was selling for £3.15 a bushel, plus six pence a mile for carriage. The salt shortage also spurred land speculation. Advertisements immediately began to appear in colonial newspapers for land as "being well suited for manufacturing salt."

This was a situation that must at once have appealed to a speculator like Robert Murray, who had already spotted the money-making potential of mining in a wartime situation. So the family plunged into the business of manufacturing salt. Lindley and his father posted a bond of £200 with the Provincial Congress in May 1776 for the project, and then received a grant of £100 to pursue the work. Paying £200 and getting back £100 for the work is not a great bargain, but the Murrays, wounded by the *Beulah* affair, were not in a position to be fussy.[11]

In his account, Lindley never mentions his father's name in connection with the salt project, but merely says he had a "partner." Even three decades later, he shrank from presenting the effort as a Murray family enterprise. The account of the salt works is the only instance in the *Memoirs* where Lindley attempts to cast his conduct in a patriotic light. "We embraced the scheme the more cordially," he says, "because we were attached to our country, and felt for the distresses in which it was involved." There is undoubtedly truth in this sentiment, but considering the omission of any reference to his committee work and the *Beulah* affair, there is also a lack of candor about it.

The aim, Lindley tells us, was to manufacture salt on "an island near the bay where I resided," undoubtedly Fire Island, which lies across Great South Bay from Long Island. The shallowness of Great South Bay, particularly on the Fire Island side, made it attractive for extracting bay salt. The idea for making bay salt may have come from an article in March 1776 in the *Pennsylvania Magazine*, a publication that the Murrays, with their close Philadelphia connections, would certainly have known. Or they may have learned about it from a reprint distributed by the Continental Congress. The article, an extract of a longer work by William Brownrigg, a fellow of the Royal Society, specifically dealt with the making of bay salt in America.

At any rate, Lindley proceeded with the work. "We procured materials at a considerable expense," he says, "employed artificers to construct the works, and were just ready to begin the manufacture, and reap the fruit of our labors, when the British forces took possession of New York, and consequently of Long Island. This event entirely superseded our operations; as the article of salt was then abundantly introduced into the country. Our loss was considerable."[12]

The failure of the salt venture also provides the reader with an explanation for Lindley's next move, as described in the *Memoirs*. "In the wake of this setback, and because I perceived the necessity of doing something that would provide permanent funds for the expenses of my family," Lindley says he decided to return to the city. According to Lindley's account, it was Robert Murray who persuaded him to return in 1779 and take up trade, implying that he had not been involved in other commerce at all during his years on Long Island.[13]

The idea of Lindley as an obedient, neutral Quaker withdrawing to Long Island away from the bellicose fray, which has been accepted by several commentators, is suspect. This is a man who before and during the *Beulah* affair had staunchly refused to bow to serious pressure by the New York Meeting for Sufferings to drop his role on "publick committees." But there are other reasons to question Lindley's version of his Long Island stay.

An item appearing in Hugh Gaine's newspaper, the *New York Mercury*, on June 15, 1778, read as follows: "Friday, 5th inst., Eben. Dayton, with 6 others took Mr. McIntire's sloop whilst they lay near Blue Pt., and stripped a sloop of Lindley Murray." This is certainly the vessel referred to by Lindley Murray in the *Memoirs*. After his move to Long Island, he says, "I purchased a very convenient, little pleasure-boat." The characterization "little pleasure-boat" seems a clear denial 30 years later by Lindley, as the *Memoirs* were being written, that his vessel had been used for commerce.[14]

The Ebeneezer Dayton who stripped Lindley's sloop was a prominent Suffolk County patriot. He had been a captain and quartermaster of the Minute Men Regiment raised in Suffolk County to oppose the British before the Battle of Brooklyn. With the British conquest of Long Island, he had fled to Connecticut. From there, he took to raiding British or pro-British shipping on the Long Island coast.[15]

As a Suffolk man, Dayton would have been familiar with the residents and their political sympathies and activities in the sparsely settled county. It is not likely he would have raided the vessel of a person favorable to the patriot cause or indeed someone who was genuinely neutral. There were targets enough among those the patriots considered enemies. The fact that Lindley Murray's sloop was considered fair game by Drayton almost certainly meant it was doing work perceived to be favorable to the British.

Drayton's 1778 raid is not the only bit of evidence pointing to Lindley's involvement in trading with the British on Long Island.

A 1779 letter from General Alexander McDougall to Governor George Clinton of New York refers to a plot to get supplies to the British troops, presumably those garrisoning Long Island. "Robert Murray is on Long Island," says McDougall, "with a store of goods, which makes one link of the chain." McDougall's charge that the Robert Murray firm was involved, presumably with Lindley as its agent, throws light on why Drayton may have made Lindley's boat a target.[16]

Other questions arise about Lindley's time on Long Island, if we examine his account in the *Memoirs*. He presents the failure of the salt project as a reason for returning to the city in 1779. But the salt project—purportedly meant to aid the patriots—was a dead letter by September 1776 when the British occupied Long Island after the Battle of Brooklyn.

Yet another reason for the return to New York, Lindley says, was that the "British power was still maintained at New York, and appeared likely to be established there." In fact, to any sensible observer at the time, British power would have seemed much more solid in the fall of 1776 after the occupation of New York, than in 1779. So why didn't Lindley return in 1776? An occupation with family business seems to be the most likely answer. In addition to the *Beulah* affair, Lindley's activities on Long Island seem another reason why he was exiled a half-decade later.

There is something else. Lindley never mentions that it was becoming dangerous for him to remain where he was. Suffolk County was largely pro-patriot, and it had become well-nigh impossible for the British to protect their sympathizers on Long Island. There was simply too much territory and coastline for the British and their German mercenaries (who did much of the military work on Long Island) to defend. It was a conflict in which it was impossible not to take sides, and each side knew the political sympathies of every person and household. Raids like Drayton's were a common occurrence and Tories were constantly being harassed and even killed by marauding patriots.[17]

The feelings in Long Island, particularly for suspected loyalists like Lindley, must have mirrored those of residents of Westchester County, as described by one contemporary: "The people of Westchester feared everybody whom they saw and loved nobody. Fear was the only passion by which they were animated."[18]

While Westchester was directly on the dividing line between the British and the Continental Army, the vulnerability of Long Island to raids from Connecticut and Rhode Island must have led to insecurity there, too. The presence of patriot raiders on Long Island was a more likely reason for driving Lindley back to the safety of the city than the lure of trade.

That lure was, however, not insignificant. For the Murrays, there was once again a war to profit from, but this time there was a large army headquartered in New York to add to the commercial possibilities. And competition was less because many merchants friendly to the patriot cause had fled the city. Robert paid for a cargo of imports to set his son up in business.

Robert's decision to set Lindley up in business in New York City may also have been influenced to an extent by two changes in British policy. Initially, acting under Parliament's Prohibitory Act of January 1, 1776, the British occupation authorities had halted exports from ports they controlled. By the summer of 1778, 261 merchant ships aggregating 35,000 tons were backed up in New York harbor and warehouses were packed with merchandise awaiting export. The authorities, realizing the goods were needed in Britain, permitted these vessels to depart as of September 26, 1778.

In addition, on January 1, 1779, the British military turned the city's piers, occupied without paying any wharfage since the army's capture of the city, back to their owners. These two measures opened possibilities for trade. Once Lindley returned to the city, ships carrying his goods no doubt helped cover the upkeep of the Murray wharf. After his return, Lindley lived at 209 Water Street, not far from the pier.[19]

Whenever exactly he took up trade, and however the business was managed, the decision to become an active trader with the British certainly confirmed Lindley's status in the eyes of many patriots, dating back to the *Beulah* affair, as an ally of the enemy. This verdict on Lindley's loyalism has been echoed in following generations. Lorenzo Sabine, in his important compendium of short biographies of loyalists originally published in 1864, but based on interviews of the Murrays' contemporaries such as John Jay, included Lindley Murray and his father Robert, but significantly—as noted—not his Uncle John.[20]

Once reestablished in New York City, Lindley found fertile ground for his trading activities. The British occupation, with an officer corps accustomed to high living, had brought prosperity to New York merchants. In addition, wealthy loyalists from upstate New York and other colonies fled to New York to be under British protection. There was much stylish entertaining between them and the army. Demand for provisions was so strong that at times there were food shortages. In addition, the British were doing some rebuilding of the city in the wake of a disastrous fire that had swept it soon after their arrival.[21] During these few years, Lindley Murray made a fortune—enough money to live comfortably for the rest of his life.

But on the battlefield, things had deteriorated for the British. On October 19, 1781, General Cornwallis accepted surrender terms at Yorktown, ending the military phase of the American Revolution. The news reached New York City on November 24. The British recognized the independence of the United States under the Treaty of Paris on September 3, 1783.

Before then, even the staunchest Tories realized the situation had changed dramatically. Oliver De Lancey, now an adjutant general with the British army, took steps as early as February 27, 1783, to restore seized real estate within British lines to the proper owners. Governor Tryon departed from New York City on April 15, 1783, leaving the problems of evacuation to the British military authorities.

75

Not only had the British seized a great deal of property, they had never paid for merchandise captured when the city was taken. The city had suffered numerous fires during the occupation. Its churches had been used for barracks, hospitals and stables, and were left in filthy condition. Only the Episcopal, Methodist and Moravian churches escaped requisitioning. In addition, the British had horribly mistreated American prisoners held on prison ships in New York Harbor. Some 11,000 died. The terms of the Treaty of Paris also caused ill feeling. The treaty language seemed to promise that Tories would be spared retribution and that Tory property which had been seized would be returned.

The British army, perhaps in an effort to protect its supporters, dragged out negotiations on the evacuation of the city. The British did not sail until November 25, 1783. Before leaving, some British officers, rubbing salt in the wounds of occupation, rented out the confiscated houses of Whigs to pocket a few extra pounds. Soon after the evacuation, the Continental army under Washington occupied the city.[22]

3

WHAT WAS THE MURRAYS' POSITION in New York as the fateful year 1784 began?

Robert Murray's main investment, the merchant firm of Murray & Sansom, was doing business as usual out of its premises at 184 Queen Street. At the same time, Robert and his brother maintained the partnership of Robert and John Murray, which owned retail stores and did other domestic business. All through these months of crisis, Murray & Sansom inserted regular advertisements in the family's favored newspaper, *The New York Packet*, which was owned by Samuel Loudon, an opponent of the patriot cause. (The Murrays never advertised in the Whig paper, Holt's *New York Journal*). The advertisements show a business that continued the family's traditional interests.

The most important part of that business was its trading component. Ships such as the *Edward*, the *Hannah* and the *Betsey*, in which the Murrays likely had full or partial ownership, brought goods from London and Bristol to sell in the New York store. These goods included tea, Chester and Gloucester cheese, stationery, pewter, shoes, Irish linen, hats, silver watches, wool and a range of other fabrics. In addition, Murray & Sansom imported spirits from Jamaica in the brig *Mary* and sugar from Havana. The Murrays' interest in the Hibernia mine apparently continued because another frequently advertised Murray & Sansom line included pig iron and cast iron items.[23]

Despite this continuing trade, however, the months that followed were a dangerous time for the Murrays, who had already been the target of patriot agitators before the Revolution. After all, Robert Murray owned a company with a London branch, had recently resided in Britain for a number of years, and had signed a petition of welcome to the British Army after the occupation of New York. Not only had his property been spared from seizure by the British authorities, but Inclenberg during the occupation had been a favorite gathering place for British officers.[24]

At first, however, there was not much change in life in New York City following the British evacuation, as Washington's troops under Henry Knox maintained order. Lindley Murray, apparently hoping his wartime activities would be overlooked, took over an estate near his father's owned by the merchant Peter Keteltas. The mansion of the property was located near the East River at what is today Twenty-Fifth Street.[25] The estate was called Bellevue, and is today remembered in the name of Bellevue Hospital in New York, which is on the site. Lindley also continued his family duties. On January 4, 1784, along with his brother John, he was a witness to a codicil of the will of Samuel Bowne, uncle of Lindley's wife Hannah Dobson.[26]

Then, as the weeks passed into months after the British withdrawal, more and more Whigs returned from exile to the city, and of course sentiment grew against those who had collaborated with the British. The anger was fueled by a multitude of complaints. "Tories," one commentator explains, "had held their city for seven years, had taken their jobs, had lived in their houses, and had farmed their land."[27]

For loyalists, there were widespread physical intimidation and continual threats of banishment. Newspaper advertisements, signed "Whigs," excoriated merchants who had done business with the British.[28] Given the high feelings, it is amazing that there were no murders of loyalists; rather, the patriots, now in control of state and city politics, seemed to put much of their energy into seeking legislative and administrative relief.[29]

Quondam enemies of the Murray family were now in positions of power. Alexander McDougall, for example, critical of the family's activities during the war, was elected to the Continental Congress early in the year and as a state senator in the spring of 1784. The Murrays' status as Quakers may have provided some minimal mitigation for their wartime conduct. But while Americans were forgiving of Quakers who remained genuinely neutral in the war, Lindley Murray had been a profiteer servicing the occupying British, and Robert had been treated with favoritism by the occupiers. And, of course, the *Beulah* affair was etched into public consciousness.

Pressure on collaborators grew during 1784, and the Sons of Liberty set May 1 as a cutoff date for offenders to depart the city or face the consequences.[30] On May 12, the state legislature passed an act that permitted 27 loyalists to return to the state. Given the position of the Murrays, there were no doubt similar attempts to obtain a clean bill of health for Lindley. To remain in New York City, however, was impossible.

Lindley finished off one bit of business for the New York Friends. After returning from Long Island, Lindley had taken an interest in the founding of a new school, which was to become Friends Seminary in New York, which continues to this day. On May 26, he submitted to the New York Preparative Meeting a report on behalf of the "Committee for the Superintending of Friends School." In it he said: "Agreeable to our Appointment, we have contracted with a Schoolmaster [to] open the School."[31] (Even after his exile to England, Lindley remained on the board of trustees of the new school. His brother John was also a member. Robert Murray gave £200 for the founding of the school, which opened in 1786.)[32]

But now it was prudent for Lindley to remove himself from the political passions of the city. As usual, he gives health as a reason for his departure. Lindley's choices of destinations for his interior exile, as related in the *Memoirs*, are revealing. First he moved to the Friends' stronghold of Bristol, Pennsylvania, across the river from Burlington, New Jersey, where he had gone to learn French. Then he went to take the waters in the remote New Jersey mountains. Finally, he traveled to Bethlehem, Pennsylvania, headquarters of the Moravian sect, spending several weeks there.[33] And what characteristic do the Moravians share with the Friends? They are both pacifist groups. Indeed, New York Moravians, faced with a situation similar to that faced by Quakers during the British occupation, had in fact gained a reputation as loyalists. Bethlehem was a place where no one was going to dark Lindley Murray about his wartime activities.

There was another circumstance that likely was instrumental in drawing Lindley to Bethlehem. Jacob Van Vleck, also the son of a prominent New York merchant and undoubtedly an acquaintance of Lindley's, was in Bethlehem at this time. A rising figure in the Moravian Church (and later a bishop), he was superintendent of the Moravian Brethren's House in Bethlehem.[34]

From his description, Lindley seems almost lyrically happy in the sylvan surroundings of Moravian country. In one passage, Lindley describes a charming encounter with a group of some 30 young women on a berry-picking expedition in the country, indicating the time of year was probably late May or early June. The girls were no doubt pupils and staff from the well-known Moravian boarding school for girls in Bethlehem.[35]

Over three decades later, Lindley's brother John (also perhaps drawn by the presence of Jacob Van Vleck) visited the Moravian area on a holiday with his family and wrote to Lindley about it. Replying, Lindley recalled his own stay in the area with Hannah. "We spent several weeks at this pleasant spot," he says, "a little before we left our native shores: and our dear father and sister Beulah came to us at that place a few days before we left it. If you recollected that circumstance, when you were at Bethlehem, I think it must have excited emotions of an affectionate and profitable nature, associations and reflections on the transient enjoyments and connexions of time."[36] The emotion-laden language and poignant evocation of "transient enjoyments and connexions of time" underline the importance of his visit to Moravian country for Lindley.

During or soon after berry-picking time, Lindley's father visited him in Pennsylvania. Apparently, he brought the sad news that all roads were now closed, and in an arrangement with the political authorities to protect the family property from seizure, Lindley would be forced into exile abroad. (The probable ingredients in such a settlement are discussed below.)

Despite the legislative act allowing some loyalists to return, anger against them persisted. Among those who voted against the the law was Alexander McDougall, who had had such anxiety about the effects of the *Beulah* affair. McDougall and his allies argued that those who supported the British war effort should not be allowed back into New York at all.[37]

Together, Robert and his son returned from Moravian country to New York. Several months later, having settled his affairs, Lindley became one of the thousands of post-Revolution loyalist boat people. His description of his departure in the *Memoirs* is truly touching:

> Soon after the determination was made, we prepared for the voyage. The trying scene now commenced of taking leave of our relations and friends. Many of them accompanied us to the ship, in the cabin of which we had a most solemn part-

ing. An eminent minister was present at the time, for whom we had a particular esteem and regard, and who prayed fervently on the occasion. It was a deeply affecting time... Our feelings, at the moment of separation, may be more easily conceived than described... With many, if not all of those beloved connexions, we parted never to see them again, in this life.[38]

The eminent minister mentioned was Lindley Murray's cousin, Jacob Lindley of Philadelphia, who had gained renown as a Quaker emissary to the Indians. He recalled the deeply emotional scene more than 25 years later. "I have often recurred," says Jacob in a letter to Lindley's brother John, "to the sensations attending my mind at the truly affecting season of his departure in the Cabin of the Vessel."[39]

The ship that would carry Lindley and Hannah Murray to the port of Lymington, near the Isle of Wight, was undoubtedly the *Betsey*, owned by the firm of Murray & Sansom, which left New York about December 1, 1784.[40] The voyage took, as Lindley says in the *Memoirs*, about five weeks, normal for the time. The crossing in winter, certainly not the preferred time to go, almost ended disastrously. "Near the conclusion of the voyage," Lindley recalled, "we narrowly escaped some very dangerous rocks, which would in all probability have proved fatal to us, if we had struck upon them."[41] A few days later, the couple reached London, and after a stay of five weeks proceeded to the vicinity of York, where there was a large Quaker community. Eventually, Lindley and Hannah settled in a spacious house in the suburb of Holdgate (today spelled Holgate).

The decision not to settle in London, where most exiles from New York had gone, and where there was a large Quaker community, is significant and symbolic. Lindley Murray shared none of the avid Toryism of most exiles, people like Oliver or James De Lancey, his old companion from the Debating club. And he undoubtedly wished to avoid the squabbling, recriminating life of the American exiles in London, obsessed with obtaining compensation from the British government for the property they had lost in America. Lindley Murray never applied for any such relief.

4

BUT WHY EXACTLY WAS LINDLEY FORCED to leave New York? There is no indication that he was under any threat to his person in Moravian country. He probably could have lived there indefinitely in peace. The obvious reason was to forestall possible confiscation of the Murray family's property in New York. The Murrays must have been very fearful of such seizure. Acquaintances of theirs such as the Bayards, the De Lanceys and the Lows were among those who had already had their estates seized by the state legislature under the Confiscation Act of 1779.[42]

There were at least two confiscations among many that must have honed the fears of Robert and Lindley. The committee on confiscation had sold the 330-acre family homestead of Judge Daniel Kissam at auction; the auctioneer was Alexander McDougall himself.[43] Daniel Kissam was the cousin of Benjamin Kissam, Robert Murray's counselor and the lawyer in whose office Lindley Murray and John Jay had trained. This happened even though Benjamin Kissam had been a supporter of the patriot cause and was the best friend of the influential Jay.

Even closer to the bosom of the Murray family was the case of John Lindley of North Carolina, a grandson of James Lindley, Jr., and thus a second cousin of Lindley Murray. He was undoubtedly well known to the Murrays of New York because of their stay in North Carolina in the early 1750s. Late in the Revolution, this John Lindley was arrested as a Tory in Chatham County, North Carolina, was subsequently deprived of *all* his property and driven into exile from the colony in 1782.

For the Murrays, who had worked so hard to obtain worldly goods and valued them highly, the fate of John Lindley of North Carolina was a terrifying example of what could happen in the wake of the Revolution. Though John Lindley was subsequently allowed to return to North Carolina, he was apparently impoverished.[44]

While there are no documents from this period detailing the New York Murray family's apprehensions about property seizure, there is ample evidence from a later period about the nature of Lindley's fears in 1784.

On June 22, 1807, in what has become known as the *Chesapeake* affair, one step leading to the War of 1812, the U.S. frigate *Chesapeake* was seized just outside American territorial waters by H.M.S. *Leopard*, which demanded the right to search for deserting British sailors. The *Chesapeake* was forced to submit to the impressment of four of her crew, two of whom were American-born. In the wake of the incident, war was in the air. There were calls for action against the United States in the British press.[45]

Lindley, who had retained his American citizenship, was not slow to read the augurs, and was at pains to make his legal status clear to his brother John. "We are somewhat alarmed with the late intelligence of an American Frigate having been captured by a British ship of war," he wrote from York, England, on August 3, 1807. "We earnestly hope it will not lead to a rupture between the two countries. . . if hostilities should take place, and confiscations, on each side, of private property should be made, I am to be considered an American; and thou will be careful to have this point settled so timely as to prevent any seizure of my property at New York."

He returned to the subject in a letter of May 2, 1808: "If my property in the New York Bank should be judged by thee and our Uncle Murray to be *unsafe*, you know you have permission given long ago, to place it where it will be *safe*. I confide in your care and judgment that in changing the situation of my property, it will not be placed in equally dangerous hands." It is evident that the three-decade old family anxiety about property seizure still affected Lindley deeply. He also communicated his conservative, not to say fearful, attitude on money matters to his wife Hannah, urging her to live only on the interest from her money. Writing to Catherine Murray in 1830, she recalled: "My *ever precious Lindley* often desired me, never to break in on the principal."[46]

Amid all the seizures of property in the wake of the Revolution, the Murrays had lost none of theirs, despite the *Beulah* affair. Everyone knew that Robert Murray had been the major villain in the affair, and that Lindley, in his actions, was only being loyal to the family. But Robert was the patriarch and was growing old—he died rather suddenly two years later. It seems evident that Lindley was a sacrificial lamb for his father's actions and had acted to protect his own and his family's property in New York City. With such pressures, the departure of Lindley was an expulsion as much as a self-exile.

In the considerable correspondence among the members of the Murray family—at least the letters that have survived—the reasons behind Lindley's departure are not directly discussed. But family members treat him with a consideration, delicacy and deference that implies that they feel they owed him a great debt. They, and in particular his younger brother John, listen without complaint to his often peremptory instructions, leap to fulfill his every demanding whim, and continually seek his advice and counsel.

There is another intriguing aspect to Lindley's departure. It seems to be one thread among many that signaled a return to normalcy in New York and an accommodation between the Whig party, now in political power in the city and state, and New York City's business community.

The continual pressure and agitation from returned patriots was a palpable fact of life in New York City in 1784. But another equally strong force was the reestablishment of normal patterns of commerce in the wake of the Revolution, developments in which the Murrays played an important part. A key organization in this regard was the New York Chamber of Commerce. Robert Murray had been one of 20 New York businessmen who met on

April 5, 1768, to establish the chamber. Its establishment was an indication that the depression of the 1760s was fully at an end. The chamber had met monthly and played an active role in New York affairs through May 2, 1775, when the onrushing events leading to the Revolution caused it to suspend activities.

With export restrictions lifted and the city's wharves returned to their owners, the chamber resumed its monthly meetings on June 21, 1779. The British, of course, still occupied the city. Robert Murray was immediately appointed to a committee to hear disputes, a position he had frequently filled in the years before the Revolution. John Murray was elected a member several weeks later, on August 3, and was soon serving on the disputes committee himself. On April 3, 1780, Robert was appointed to a fourteen-man chamber committee to draw up a new charter for the city.

On May 6, 1783, the chamber once again suspended meetings, resuming on January 20, 1784, after the British withdrawal from the city. At that meeting, both Murrays were in attendance and thirteen new members were proposed, among them Quakers such as Samuel Franklin and Murray relatives by marriage such as John Bowne and William Demming, who would naturally be sympathetic to the Murrays' position. While the newly returned Whigs may have had scores to settle with the Murrays, the city's business establishment did not, and the Murrays had bolstered support in the Chamber of Commerce, where voices could be raised on their behalf.[47]

In addition to the business community, likely support for the Murrays' position and against seizure of their property arose from the changed political climate in New York. A key figure was James Duane, who had been sworn in as mayor of New York in February 1784. Duane's country estate, Gramercy, which today includes the Gramercy Park neighborhood of Manhattan, was just south of Inclenberg. Duane had supported the patriot cause, but was very much a person of conservative views, anxious to pour oil on the troubled waters of post-Revolution New York, as well as to develop its municipal and charitable institutions.

Duane served with Robert Murray as a governor of New York Hospital, originally founded in 1771, burned down in the Revolution, and rebuilt after the war.[48] In addition, during 1784, Robert Murray was working with Mayor Duane on another public project, the Bridewell Alms House, where the city's poor (whose numbers had increased in the wake of the war) were cared for. To be sure, the poor were also closely supervised and made to work, to prevent "an idle and profligate Banditti" from continuing to "rob and steal." Murray was one of Bridewell's eleven commissioners (as were fellow Friends John and Samuel Franklin). Thanks to Duane, it was agreed that the Bridewell's staff would be paid from public funds, and provisions, bedding and firewood furnished.[49] The idea that Robert may have been serving on public committees as part of the settlement of the controversy over the Murray's property is given credence by the fact that he resigned from the committee in September 1785, after Lindley's departure.

There was another important development in 1784 that lessened friction between the Whigs who now held political power in city and state and the business community, and may well have served as a mitigating circumstance in the Murrays' case. It was the establishment of the city's first bank, the Bank of New York, which opened its doors in June 1784. The main impetus for the establishment of the bank came from businessmen led by Alexander Hamilton, but to deflect potential criticism from Whigs, its presidency was given to a former merchant who was now an influential political leader, the Murrays' old nemesis Alexander McDougall. That appointment was a symbol of the city's return to normalcy; the Murrays, including Lindley, were early purchasers of the bank's stock.[50]

Duane is the person who must have brought all these strands together. As presiding official of the mayor's court, he played the central role in questions of confiscation. It is impossible to conceive that important merchants like the Murrays would not consult with a neighbor, friend and powerful political presence such as Duane. It is probable that Duane suggested or endorsed the solution of Lindley's exile. As a patriot and as mayor, Duane was in a position to negotiate with McDougall and other Whig leaders. The agreement he helped make traded Lindley's departure for the safeguarding of the Murrays' property.

Support for the idea that Duane was the crucial intermediary comes in a letter from Lindley to Duane written from New York and dated June 10, 1784 (which would have been immediately after his return from Moravian country with his father). The three-paragraph letter does not specifically mention any negotiations, but it has the tone of a grateful thank-you note. Lindley compliments Duane for his

> Exertions for the good of thy fellow Creatures in the various Capacities under which Providence has placed thee—& I doubt not, if honestly and unswervingly pursued, they will be crown'd here with a Peace which the Honours and pleasures of this World cannot confer; & rewarded in the World to Come with a Happiness infinitely exceeding all our little Labours here, and which will know no Termination.[51]

Lindley was forced into exile for trading with the British, but he was also the scapegoat for Robert Murray's activities, including most notably the *Beulah* affair. In retrospect, at the end of the Revolution, the threat that the *Beulah* affair had posed to New York's relations with its fellow colonies must have seemed large indeed. Lindley was thrown to the wolves, but Robert was spared and seizure of Murray family property averted.

Lindley's decision to accept exile was wrenching and emotional, and though he bowed to his father's wishes with sadness, he did so without deep resentment. In a letter to Robert, written from London on March 3, 1785, after his exile, Lindley is still caught up in the vivid emotions of his departure. He bemoans

> the Loss of you in this Land, where we have scarce any Relative and not many Acquaintances; but I hope it is all in the wisdom of Providence, and that we have not been

without the care of a gracious Parent in this great
undertaking. . . let our Lott and Condition be as it may—
sure I am that there is no solid comfort for us, but what
looks beyond the Things of Time.

Lindley signs the letter "thy affectionate and dutifull Son." Until
his death two years later, Robert Murray handled all of Lindley's
affairs in America.[52]

Though driven from America as one, Lindley never thought
of himself as a loyalist. He never used the word in his letters or
books, even about others. If he had indeed felt loyalist
sympathies, it is unlikely that he would have chosen Yorkshire as
a place to live because loyalists tended to congregate in and
around London. Most important of all, he does not display in his
books even a hint of the Tory sympathies that characterize most
loyalists. As I will argue in the next chapter, he was in fact entirely
Whiggish in his sentiments and the perfect exemplar of the
Enlightenment civic humanist.

As Henry May says, writing about the exiles of this period:
"Revolutions force moderates to chose sides, and the process is
always painful. . . When the British ships sailed from Boston, then
Philadelphia, and finally Charleston and New York, a portion of
the moderate Enlightenment sailed with them."[53]

Lindley's feelings on arriving in Britain are summed up in the
Memoirs. Characteristically, he framed them in Whiggish terms.
"I knew that under this excellent government," he wrote of
Britain, "life, property, reputation, civil and religious liberty, are
happily protected."[54] He simply felt that his life, property and reputation were not safe in America at this moment in history. It is
worth noting once again that while he lived in Britain, Murray
retained American citizenship, which helped make it difficult for
anyone to seize his property in New York.

That is how Lindley Murray came to old York from New York.
The Bellevue estate was sold on March 25, 1786, to a Thomas
Smith for the substantial sum of £2,200.[55] Lindley later summed
up his situation: "When we left our native shores, we fondly sup-

posed, that in the course of two years, my health might be so established, as to enable us to return to our friends and country. This term was the utmost boundary we had assigned for our absence from home. How short-sighted is the mind of man!"[56]

The time of his exile was a tragedy for his family and a dark night of the soul for Lindley, but from the point of view of the historian, at the age of 41 his most important years—as a writer of textbooks that would affect tens of millions of pupils—still lay ahead.

5

IT IS A SHAME THAT LINDLEY MURRAY'S *MEMOIRS* help so little in understanding his last crucial years before the exile. His refusal to discuss the American Revolution is the central absurdity of the *Memoirs*. As he penned them in 1806–1809, isolated in Yorkshire, he was understandably nervous (as his correspondence reveals) about the maintenance of his property and investments in New York, upon which he depended to maintain his standard of living. The lesson of wide seizures of Tory property, including the fates of Judge Daniel Kissam and his cousin John Lindley, were still no doubt vivid in his memory, even though circumstances had changed greatly in New York.

In addition, Lindley was undoubtedly concerned with the social position of his family in New York. Throughout his years in exile, he displayed great solicitude for his brother and sisters and their children. During this entire time, the New York merchant class that emerged victorious from the Revolution had solidified its social standing, participating in prestigious patriotic groups such as the Order of the Cincinnati. It was not at all fashionable to display loyalist connections. One senses that Lindley wished to safeguard his American family from the embarrassment attached to his actions during the Revolution.

Throughout the *Memoirs*, at particularly delicate moments— his father's move to London to set up a new business, his own forced exile from New York state, his final exile to Britain—Lindley attributes the moves to questions of health. Although these were undoubtedly times of deep depression for Robert and Lindley Murray, with consequent physical effects, this invoking of health concerns to draw a veil over the realities of the situation is most charitably interpreted as a diplomatic white lie.

For example, in his *Memoirs*, Murray contends he left New York for his health and that Yorkshire was suggested by his doctor.[57] But it seems extremely odd that anyone would remove himself to Yorkshire for reasons of health, even on a temporary basis. Whatever its other virtues, Yorkshire does not have a great reputation for a salubrious climate, and indeed during the rest of his life there Lindley was constantly dogged by colds, frequently heavy ones, as well as rheumatism; his wife Hannah also contracted rheumatism.[58]

It is well to remember that Robert Murray, who supposedly went to England during the 1760s because of health, did not die until the age of 65 (of a fairly sudden heart attack or stroke). As for Lindley Murray, he undoubtedly did suffer ailments later in life, but they seem more related to rheumatism or arthritis than other causes. Even when he was of advanced age, an American visitor described his face as ruddy and animated. The supposedly sickly Lindley, let us remember, lived to be 81.

Robert Murray died in New York following his short illness in 1786, two years after Lindley's departure. In his will, he divided the moneys due from his businesses—from Murray, Sansom & Co. and from Robert and John Murray, his separate partnership with his brother—among his five children. (Uncle John Murray was to be very slow about making this payment from the partnership, a sore point with Lindley over the following decade.)

The estate at Inclenberg went to Lindley's sister Susannah. His brother John received the house where he was living at 337 Queen Street, as well as real estate "on the southerly side of Burnet's Key." Lindley received a house and lot at 155 Queen

Street. In addition, he was left his father's gold watch and "an ancient warming pan which has been in our families near two hundred years," particular acknowledgements of the great sacrifice Lindley had made to safeguard the fortune of the Murray family.[59]

Lindley Murray's
ENGLISH READER

7

DRIVEN FROM HIS NATIVE land, Lindley settled into a house in Holdgate, just outside York, and took up the life of a country gentleman, pursuing Quaker causes. Like the good Friend he was, he supported William Wilberforce in his parliamentary drive to abolish slavery. This was in keeping with a longtime family interest of the Murrays. In his will, Robert Murray had left money for the education of slaves, and Lindley's brother John was a driving force in establishing the New York Society for the Manumission of Slaves.[1]

In his exile, Lindley also began to do literary work.

In York in 1787, three years after his arrival, Lindley Murray published his first book, *The Power of Religion on the Mind in Retirement, Sickness and Death* (later retitled *The Power of Religion on the Mind in Retirement, Affliction and at the Approach of Death*). It consisted of excerpts of writings of or about well-known figures concerning death.

The first printing, done in York, was 500 copies, paid for by Murray, and distributed to friends, but later the printing was shifted to a London publisher. The book eventually went through more than twenty editions in Britain, and was translated into French.

The *Power of Religion* consists of vignettes of famous historical figures such as Confucius, Socrates, the Venerable Bede, Sir Walter Raleigh, Isaac Newton and John Locke, but also eighteenth-century figures such as Joseph Addison and Joseph

Hervey. Although there is a lugubrious, death-haunted tone to it—Lindley's father had died just a year before, and he was also obviously wrestling with the fact of his exile—*The Power of Religion* displays wide reading and an open-minded choice of subjects for vignettes. "As I wished to form it on liberal principles," Lindley wrote in the *Memoirs* "and render it acceptable to readers in general, I was careful to introduce characters of various religious professions, and of different ages and countries. The concurrence of these, in the recommendation of religion, as the great promoter of our happiness here and hereafter, would, I conceived, form a strong persuasive evidence, in the cause of piety and virtue." Although he does include some Quakers, Murray casts his net wide and even includes several Catholics, such as Cardinal Richelieu and Cardinal Mazarin.[2]

The Power of Religion proved to be the most influential of Lindley's works outside his textbooks, becoming a staple of Quaker reading well into the nineteenth century. It must have demonstrated to Lindley the efficacy of a well-chosen, wide-ranging anthology of readings, and he followed this form in compiling his reading textbooks. Strictly speaking, of course, such anthologies are not "writing," but they do provide their compiler with a coherent way to convey ideas.

Initially, the book was anonymous, but by the sixth edition Lindley had enlarged it and put his name on it. He showed a keen interest in having the book distributed in America. In his correspondence with his younger brother John in New York in these years, there is hardly an instance when he does not give instructions for the distribution of the book to family members, fellow Quakers and persons of influence.[3]

As a person of wide education and literary ability, Lindley was looked upon by his fellow Quakers in York as a resource for aiding the education of the young. At a new school established in York by Friends for the "guarded" education of young women, Murray helped train the teachers in grammar.[4] He also gave individual lessons to pupils.

Stephen Allott imagines one such scene: "On a winter evening, about the year 1790, three young Quaker women might have been seen passing out of Micklegate Bar in York, attended by a man carrying a lantern. They were on their way to the village of Holgate, a mile outside the city walls, for a lesson in grammar from the American Quaker lawyer, Lindley Murray... They came from the Quaker girls' school, established in Trinity Lane in 1784 by Esther Tuke; their lessons were the origin of Murray's English Grammar."[5]

Having had a distinct success with *The Power of Religion*, Lindley issued his *English Grammar* in 1795. It was an immediate success. He instantly became a sought-after textbook author, and the *Grammar* was followed, in 1797, by two grammar exercise books—*English Exercises* and *A Key to the Exercises*—and what was to be his very popular abridgement of the *Grammar*. In 1799, he published his *English Reader*, followed by two other readers in the next two years, and a spelling book in 1804. (The speller, which was used to teach small children to read, the *Introduction to the English Reader*, the *English Reader* and *Sequel to the English Reader* in effect formed a four-book reading series.) Murray's *First Book for Children* appeared in 1805 and two readers in French followed over the next several years. A complete revision of the *Grammar* appeared in 1818.[6]

Though Murray was a successful author in Britain, it was in the United States that he had his largest sales. Every Murray textbook published in Britain was followed soon after by its appearance in America, the road considerably smoothed by the fact that American printers did not have to pay Murray any royalties.[7] *The Power of Religion,* published by the Quaker Joseph Crukshank in Philadelphia in 1790, was the first Murray title to appear in the United States. But Murray's main publisher in the United States was to be another Quaker, Isaac Collins, a former associate of Crukshank. The first Murray volume published by Collins was an enlarged edition of *The Power of Religion,* which appeared in Trenton, New Jersey, in 1795.

Collins, now established in New York, printed the *Reader* in 1799, the first Murray textbook published in the United States. John Murray, Lindley's brother, who had been operating the family business in New York, had copyrighted both the *Grammar* and the *Exercises* in New York on December 4, 1798.[8] But Collins did not print the first New York *Grammar* until 1800, and the first New York *Exercises* not until 1801.

By 1801, the pace of Murray publications in America had picked up. In 1800 alone, ten editions of Murray textbooks—including the *Abridgement, Grammar, Reader* and *Exercises*—had been printed in New York, Boston and Philadelphia.[9] Almost immediately, the *Grammar* began to rival the established grammar text, the second part of Noah Webster's *Grammatical Institute of the English Language.*[10]

By 1810, the entire range of Murray's textbooks was being published in nearly all the major cities of the United States. They were even available on the frontier. A Kentucky almanac printed in 1809 advertises the *English Reader,* the *Introduction,* the *Sequel,* the *Grammar,* the *Abridgement,* the *Exercises* and *Key,* and the *Spelling-Book.*[11]

From 1801 through 1840, Murray's total published output of literacy textbooks in the United States was about 12.5 million copies. This total exceeds the output of Noah Webster in these years.[12] The market for these astonishing totals was the burgeoning number of schools throughout America, unmatched by any school system in the world. Including the British figures, Murray's total output of some 15.5 million copies makes him the best-selling producer of books in the world during the first four decades of the nineteenth century. (See Appendix.)

In Britain, the *Grammar* series proved the most popular of Murray's titles. But it was the *English Reader* that was by far his best-selling book in the United States. Murray's book first rivaled, then outdistanced Caleb Bingham's readers, *The American Preceptor* and *The Columbian Orator.* By 1803, Murray's *Reader* was being published in Newark, New Jersey, and by 1805 in

Brattleboro, Vermont, and Newbern, North Carolina, a Quaker stronghold.

There were 68 editions of Murray's *Reader* by 1814. But the years of glory for Murray's *Reader* were from 1815 through 1836. It completely dominated the field, with 259 American editions. Its rivals were left in the dust. (See Appendix.)

Some five million copies of the *Reader* were sold in the United States, nearly all before 1850. The other books in Murray's reading series, *Introduction to the English Reader* and *Sequel to the English Reader*, sold another one-and-a-half million copies in the same period. The complete domination of Murray's readers began to end with the appearance of the McGuffey reading series in 1836. With their larger print, pictures and stories that appealed to children, the McGuffeys almost entirely replaced the *English Reader* in the next decade.

The irony is that, despite its success in the American market, the *English Reader* does not contain a single selection by an American author. This did not escape the notice of Murray's competitors. Here is a wonderful fulmination from Lyman Cobb, author of series such the *Juvenile Readers*, the *North American Readers*, and the *New North American Readers*:

> The *English Reader* so largely used in our country does not contain a single piece or paragraph written by an American citizen. Is this good policy? Is it patriotism? Shall the children of this great nation be compelled to read, year after year, none but the speeches and writings of men whose feelings and views are in direct opposition to our institutions and government?[13]

Thus speaks a man who, commercially speaking, was being crushed by Lindley Murray. Cobb was not the only textbook writer to complain about Murray: John Pierpont and Joshua Leavitt did the same.[14]

What has been the opinion of subsequent commentators on the phenomenon of the *English Reader*? To the extent that the subject has been discussed at all, the assumption of textbook historian Ruth Miller Elson seems to be typical. "For physical and economic reasons," she says, "cultural independence took longer to achieve [than political]... English books continued to be used well into the nineteenth century."[15] Thus, it is Elson's assumption that the criticism of Lyman Cobb was correct, and that the content of the *English Reader* was somehow philosophically "British" as opposed to "American."

Both Lyman Cobb and Ruth Miller Elson were off the mark. The fact is that the *English Reader* reflected a strain of British civic humanist thought, transmitted through the Enlightenment, that had become an intrinsic part of the American intellectual landscape. That is a major reason why the Lindley Murray readers succeeded so well in the United States.

And, of course, given its success, it would be amazing if the opposite were the case, and that the *English Reader* contained any Tory ideas or Tory propaganda. If that were true, its rivals in the intensely competitive American textbook publishing world would have torn it to pieces. Americans of the time remembered their struggles with Britain and the War of 1812. We have seen how Lyman Cobb fulminated, but he was unable to point to any specific instances of anti-American content in the *English Reader*, and could only resort to unfair generalizations in attacking it.

The *English Reader* is an anthology of selections intended for children who have already learned to read. The book is divided into two parts, "Pieces in Prose" and "Pieces in Poetry," selected from prominent authors. (Though the focus in the following discussion is on the prose selections, an argument could likewise be made from the poetry selections.)[16] More than two-thirds of the book's overall space is devoted to prose, and it is in these 81 selections that the civic humanist message of the *English Reader* is most forcefully presented.

Perhaps the most remarkable thing about the book is what it does not contain. Here we have a person who, though an

American Quaker by origin, had settled down as an English country gentleman, compiling a book to be published in the first instance in Britain. Yet there is not a breath, not a hint, of Tory political philosophy in the selections in the *English Reader*. There is not a line of support for the British political system or the House of Hanover. There is absolutely no endorsement of the class system and not a single slighting reference to the lower classes. Indeed, the wealthy and powerful are basically seen in selections where they appear as villains or unhappy people, not persons to be in any way admired.

While none of the selections is in any way anti-civic humanist, 25 of the 81 prose selections in the *English Reader* can arguably be said to have specific civic humanist/Enlightenment themes, such as:

—the abuse of power by tyrants, kings and corrupt public servants;

—the power of the individual against tyranny;

—the natural equality of persons under Providence;

—the importance of individual liberty in lifting servility and subjugation;

—the importance of equal justice for all;

—the importance of integrity and "zealousness for the public interest";

—and even the ability of a simple citizen to become a virtuous ruler.[17]

The thrust of this argument is best seen in an accumulation of examples from the *Reader*. But a typical instance is Cicero's oration against Verres, where he condemns Verres for being a corrupt public servant and ignoring the rights of the citizenry: "O liberty!—O sound once delightful to every Roman ear!— once sacred—now trampled upon!"[18]

Another selection in the *English Reader*, from David Hume's *History of England*, is the story of the accomplished Lady Jane

Grey, cruelly put to death by Bloody Mary. Yet another is the speech of Adherbal to the Roman Senate, taken from the Roman historian Sallust, which condemns the violence and cruelty of tyrannical kingship.[19] Along with numerous other similar stories in the *English Reader*, the message is clear: irresponsible monarchical and tyrannical power is brought into question.

Of the authors that Murray selected for the *English Reader* some, such as Addison (nine selections), Goldsmith (six selections) and Dr. Samuel Johnson (three selections), were included in many contemporary British anthologies of readings.[20] But the great majority of contributors are of a different sort—part of a loose grouping known to history as the Commonwealthmen, a collection of eighteenth-century Whigs, republicans, reformers, Nonconformists and political dissidents. Some supported the struggle of the American colonists against the Crown and some did not, but their ideas exerted a great influence on the thinking of the people who wrote the Declaration of Independence and made the American Revolution.[21]

Among the most important of the Commonwealthmen were the writers and scholars we associate with the Scottish Enlightenment. Scottish Enlightenment figures, including David Hume, John Home, James Beattie and William Robertson, are all represented in the *English Reader*.[22] It is precisely the message of Scottish humanism that made the book so acceptable in America and distinguished Murray's reading texts from their competitors.

The largest single contributor to the *English Reader*, with 36 of the book's 81 prose selections—44 percent of the total—is a Scottish Enlightenment figure, the Rev. Hugh Blair. Blair was a literary man, a renowned preacher, and the Professor of Rhetoric and Belles Lettres at the University of Edinburgh. Blair's ideas coincide closely with those of Lindley Murray. They both have an allegiance to civic humanist politics and non-Calvinist Christian piety, and they share the Scottish Enlightenment's concern with the development of a "moral sense" in opposition to Calvinist doctrines.[23]

Blair became widely known after he was appointed preacher at the High Kirk of St. Giles, the seat of the Church of Scotland in Edinburgh. He had been a member of the Moderate party in the Church of Scotland, which had defeated the conservatives, the Calvinist so-called High Flyers, and had taken control of the Church's General Assembly. Blair's sermons were the opposite of the long, heavily Scripture-based discourses favored by the High Flyers. Rather, his sermons were well-ordered and short, and according to one commentator, "dissolved one grain of the Gospel in a cooling draught of moral disqusition."[24]

One factor that might have attracted Murray to Blair and the Moderates was their position on the events leading up to the American Revolution (as well as on the Revolution itself), which agreed with his own. William Robertson, leader of the Moderates and principal of Edinburgh University from 1762 to 1793, opposed (like the merchants of New York) the Stamp Act. In a letter of 1766, he expressed happiness about Parliament's decision to repeal the Act, adding that now "a million men of America have some chance of running the same great career which other free men have held before them."[25]

But Robertson also insisted that the colonists must be an integral part of the British system, and a decade later, he was advocating military action against the colonies.[26] Opponents of the Moderates who had emigrated to America, such as John Witherspoon of Princeton University, were, in contrast, supporters of the American Revolution. Blair, for his part, shared the Moderate position concerning the colonies.

With a boost from Dr. Samuel Johnson, the first volume of Blair's sermons was published in 1777. It was an immediate success, and over the next years, until his death at the end of 1800, Blair published another four volumes, all to applause and good sales. Blair's sermons, says David Daiches, "spoke for a humane Christianity with emphasis on the good heart and good works."[27] It was these sermons, steeped in the anti-Calvinist sentiments of Scottish humanism, that Lindley Murray mined for the selections in the *English Reader*.

In the spectrum of thought of the Scottish Enlightenment, Blair's position emphasized the uplifting possibilities of literature and the creation—replacing the dictates of Calvinism—of "good taste and the polite style." Blair put forth this view most forcefully in his influential *Lectures on Rhetoric and Belles Lettres* (1783). Here, according to one authority, "Blair subordinates rhetoric in its classical sense of political discourse to the study of polite literature," thus avoiding "the controversies of contemporary politics."[28]

So Blair provided the perfect exemplar for Lindley Murray, wrestling as he was with bitter exile from his birthplace, while trying to remain faithful to the ideals of his Enlightenment upbringing and Quaker heritage. On the one hand, Blair epitomizes Murray's view of what was best in Enlightenment and civic humanist thought. On the other hand, Blair's literary approach sidesteps the framing of civic humanist concerns in the bald political terms employed by the radicals who made the American Revolution and caused Murray's exile.

Blair seemed pleased when Murray sent the 83-year-old preacher copies of the *English Reader* and his other works in 1800, the last year of Blair's life. "I could bestow much praise for the judiciousness and propriety of the Selection, were it not that my own writings are honoured with so great a place," he wrote on October 21. Murray had made his choice of Blair excerpts without consulting the Scotsman: "As we have not much intercourse with York," said Blair, "and as I have no correspondent in that city, your name was unknown to me till I received the present of your books." Certainly, though, Blair felt Murray's choices in the *English Reader* were a fair representation of his positions.[29]

In addition to its civic humanist character and its anti-Calvinism, the thought of Hugh Blair, transmitted through the numerous excerpts in the *English Reader* and through Blair's *Lectures on Rhetoric and Belles Lettres*, fits into the American intellectual landscape of the era in another manner.

A great influence on Blair's approach to the world was Francis Hutcheson, whom many scholars see as launching the Scottish Enlightenment with his 1725 book, *Inquiry into the Original of Our Ideas of Beauty and Virtue.* "Moral goodness," says Hutcheson, "denotes an idea of some quality, apprehended in actions, which procures approbation and love toward the actor from those who receive no advantage by the action. Moral evil denotes an idea of contrary quality."[30]

That cast of thought seems to be central to Lindley Murray's method as *auteur* of the *English Reader.* In his selections, Murray wants to edify the reader by presenting good actions and paeans to virtue, and to juxtapose them against bad actions and examples of vanity, folly, pride, lust for power and so forth. There is also much praise for the concept of virtue itself, set either in no particular religious context or in a non-Calvinist Christian context.

This "moral sense" point of view is also linked to the promotion of genteel culture, another goal of the creators of the Scottish Enlightenment. The establishment of genteel culture was also a great concern of many Americans in the eighteenth century, and in the nineteenth, particularly at a time when the *English Reader* was at its most influential, from 1815 to about 1840. The ideas in the *English Reader* also mesh intellectually with the kind of "moral sense" anti-Calvinism that was developing, for instance, in the Unitarian and Transcendentalist movements in the United States. It is not my purpose in this book to delve into the transmission of Scottish Enlightenment ideas after 1800, but I suggest scholars will miss the mark if they do not give serious consideration to the role of Murray's *English Reader* in the process.

Though this analysis has concentrated on the *English Reader,* many of the same points could be made about Murray's other readers, the *Introduction to the English Reader* and the *Sequel to the English Reader.* Many of the authors are the same, including Blair. If anything, the *Introduction* is even more anti-slavery, with one of its selections devoted explicitly to condemning it.[31]

Other reading texts available in America were also anti-slavery, but the *English Reader* holds a special place because of its immense circulation, particularly from 1815 through 1840 (see Appendix). It so dominated the market that it seems likely that a large majority of American adults in the North who reached their fortieth year from 1845 through 1866 were raised on selections from the *English Reader*. One of them, as has been noted, was Abraham Lincoln, who called the *Reader* "the best schoolbook ever put in the hands of an American youth."[32]

The *English Reader* provides a clear link between the thought of mid-nineteenth century Americans and the Scottish Enlightenment of a century or more before. In its pages, the civic humanist and anti-slavery messages of French Enlightenment savants and Scottish humanists found a place in the American classroom of the antebellum United States.[33] At the same time, the *English Reader's* civic humanism helps explain why the book was not a rampant success in monarchical Britain.

Other Murrays, Other Stories

8

LINDLEY MURRAY WAS GONE, living in his house in Holdgate, but in New York life went on for the Murray family. Robert Murray was still the uncontested head of the clan, pursuing the life of a prosperous merchant, ever alert for small advantages. In 1784, Robert still held a long-term lease on the land on which Inclenberg sat. Perhaps emboldened by the ascension of his neighbor James Duane to the mayoralty, Robert proposed to the Common Council an abatement of the rent due to the city on the Inclenberg land—but the idea was rejected.[1]

Robert also continued to expand his business, and to toy with new—and even potentially dangerous—money-making schemes. He bought from the estate of John Groesbeeck land that he had been renting since 1775. The plot was adjacent to his own property on the East River. On April 20, 1785, a Common Council committee reported that "Robert Murray is willing to erect a powder magazine on his land." Presumably, this was something the municipality felt it needed, but other citizens were unwilling to allow on their own property. Thus, the same committee was directed "to confer with Mr. Murray & report his Conditions."[2] The subject is then dropped in the Common Council records, indicating that no agreement was reached.

The offer to discuss the powder magazine seems to have been part of other negotiations that Robert was conducting with the city about reduction of taxes and an expansion of his wharf. On

March 29, 1786, this entry appears in the Common Council records: "A Petition of Robert Murray relative to the Quit Rent & Wharfage of his Water Lot at the West End of Burnet's Key was read & rejected."[3]

The entire negotiation is an example of the kind of give-and-take that all major merchants would have been continually conducting with municipal officials. On the one hand, the Council's willingness to deal with Robert Murray for the apparent benefit of the city points to the de facto peace that was coming into place between the patriot-controlled government and a merchant community that had been largely pro-Crown. But in this case, the suspicions of the patriot Council concerning the man who spawned the *Beulah* affair undoubtedly made it difficult for Robert Murray to gain acceptance for his plans.

Other Murrays—Robert's brother John and Robert's son John—were also active in New York City commerce. Since both were prominent, there was often confusion between the two John Murrays. To make matters clear, John the son began styling himself John Junior to distinguish himself from his uncle. New Yorkers, however, had their own method of identifying them. Since Uncle John continued to retain his Presbyterian allegiance and was prominent in church affairs as a vestryman of the First Presbyterian Church, he became popularly known as Presbyterian John. Robert's son, John Junior, a devout and active Friend, was dubbed Quaker John.

However, John Junior did not reveal the change in the style of his name to Lindley until decades later, perhaps fearing his brother's disapproval. On one occasion, John Junior made a slip and his brother reacted immediately. In a letter of September 30, 1815, Lindley asks peremptorily, "What is my brother's reason for signing his name John Murray *Junr*, when he is in fact *senior*?"[4] Behind this complaint was a certain tension that seems to have arisen over the years between Lindley and his uncle John.

Though he always treated his uncle with proper deference, Lindley's relations with him were cooler than with others in his family. The root of the problem probably went back to the days of the Revolution and John's pro-patriot activities. There is no recorded correspondence between Lindley (who wrote constantly to many family members) and his uncle. Lindley left it to his brother to deal with Presbyterian John.

One incident that added to the strain was Uncle John's handling of estate matters in the wake of the death of Robert Murray on July 22, 1786. Uncle John, John Junior, and Lindley were the three executors of the will. Robert's death meant a dissolution of both Murray family businesses—the international trading firm of Murray & Sansom (in which Uncle John was a partner) and the domestic merchant business called Robert and John Murray. Nine days after Robert's death, the following notice appeared in New York newspapers: "The partnership of Murray, Sansom & Co. is dissolved by the death of Robert Murray. John Murray is the only person in America authorized to settle their affairs. Business will be transacted as usual under the firm Murray & Sansom."[5] Murray & Sansom did in fact continue operating for several more decades with Uncle John as its American partner.

Despite this prompt notice, and even though he was an executor, Uncle John was dilatory in distributing the monies due from the dissolved firms to the estate of Robert Murray. Matters were still unresolved six years later, and in a letter of October 1792, Lindley urged his brother to confront their uncle "respecting the 20, and 10,000 [pounds] and our expectations." Lindley brought up the subject again four months later: "I well remember hearing dear Father often saying there would be a considerable Balance coming to him or his Estate from that Firm [probably Robert and John Murray]. From these Hints you must, I think, see the consequence of having the accts. of that Concern clearly adjusted, and the exact Balance settled. . . and how it comes to pass that you have been so easy about it, I am entirely at a loss to judge: since the Transaction is an old one, and every requisite must be in Uncles Possession."[6]

Lindley's anger reflects the continual frustration he must have felt in his exile as he tried to keep up with the family's business affairs in New York, in touch only by letter. Any reply to a question took, at best, two months. Uncle John was certainly in the wrong, but John Junior had the burden of dealing with him personally on what was likely almost a daily basis. They lived near each other on Queen Street (now Pearl Street) and probably had business dealings together. Lindley was out of touch with these quotidian family realities.

At the same time, Lindley's prodding seems eventually to have had an effect, and Uncle John acted to make some settlement of the matter, considerably reducing the debt owed to Robert Murray's estate. In September 1795, Lindley writes to his brother: "I am surprised to find any debt, especially of £1000, remains unpaid by Uncle, and I wonder how you can be easy with it."[7] The subject is afterwards dropped in Lindley's correspondence, suggesting the debt had been completely satisfied.

Presbyterian John's business interests followed the family tradition. He was a partner in Murray & Sansom and had his own domestic firm, John Murray & Sons. (The sons were John R. Murray and William Ogden, actually a son-in-law). But as time passed, Presbyterian John became more and more involved with the growth of banking in New York. The Murrays had backed the Bank of New York since it opened in 1784.[8] Lindley Murray was also an early and heavy investor in the Bank of New York.[9]

Robert Bowne, related to the Murrays through Quaker John's marriage to Catherine Bowne, was a director of the bank from 1784 to 1792. Presbyterian John Murray was a director from 1780 to 1793.[10] In 1804 he became a director of the United States Bank.[11] John also was elected president of the New York Chamber of Commerce in 1798 and served until 1806, when he declined office.

Quaker John was not part of the main family business. Before the Revolution, he had opened a brewery (a profession followed by many Friends), which continued in business for decades supplying the city's numerous taverns.[12] It was located at 13 Oliver Street and in 1803 was extended through to Catherine Street. Supposedly, Gen. George Washington drank ale from Quaker John's brewery during his time in New York in the Revolution.[13] Some time after, the firm operated under the name Murray & Cunningham; the partner was a relative of the Murrays.[14] Decades later, an enthusiastic quaffer recalled the hearty drink produced by the Murray brewery and contrasted it with the lighter style of beer subsequently introduced by German immigrants: "The ale from that time-stained brewery," he wrote, "is ale. One porter mug full of that is more precious than a big Missouri river full of lager."[15]

As has been noted, Robert Murray, the man who started it all, died in July 1786. Lindley explains in the *Memoirs* that about four weeks before his death, Robert had been confined to his room complaining "of pain in his head and breast, and that his cough grew more difficult and painful."[16] The involvement of the chest and head seems to point to heart and/or circulatory problems. Robert was about 65 years old.

Robert Murray, whose wife, Mary Lindley Murray, had died in 1780, divided his estate among his progeny. He had five surviving children—Lindley, Mary, John, Beulah (who gave her name to the fateful ship of the *Beulah* affair) and Susannah.

The Inclenberg property went to Susannah, the youngest daughter, born in 1763, eighteen years after Lindley. Reputedly a great beauty, Susannah had been wooed and won in New York by Capt. Gilbert Colden Willett, a physician and member of the King's loyal American forces. In his will, Robert Murray treated Susannah with great generosity, giving her not only Inclenberg, but a parcel of land in the heart of the city in the neighborhood known as Golden Hill (the area around today's Gold, John and Fulton Streets).

Robert Murray had never actually bought the Inclenberg land from the city—it had always been leased. In February 1799,

Gilbert Colden Willett did buy it.[17] At the time, Willett was involved in a business called Willett & Murray, apparently with Presbyterian John as a partner. The business failed. Exactly what happened is not known, but business failure and bankruptcy were matters of greater gravity in the eighteenth century than today. Gilbert Colden Willett was described by a descendant as someone "distinguished in the literary world—a philosopher, a Statesman," i.e. a person with many interests outside of business and one who probably lived above his income.[18] The matter is treated with almost a hushed tone in the Murray family correspondence, so much so that one suspects that Willett may not have dealt with his partner with complete rectitude. At any rate, in the settlement Inclenberg was handed over completely to Presbyterian John in January 1800.

Gilbert Colden Willett was not able to reestablish himself after his business failure. A few years later, Lindley and the two John Murrays bought a farm and stone cottage at Coldenham, New York, up the Hudson River, for £1,100, and offered to rent it on favorable terms to the Willetts. It was a solution that not only provided a farming income but got Gilbert out of the city.

In a letter of 1805 to his sister Susannah, Lindley treated the matter with great delicacy. He tells Susannah he would be obliged to the Willetts if they would take on the farm "because I have no means of improving my property. . . All things considered, it appears to me to be the most eligible plan of life offered for my dear brother who, I understand, is attached to the country life, and likely to succeed in agriculture. . . thou hast not lost everything in leaving the city; many domestic comforts remain; and some choice society."

Lindley adds that he is sending her "one hundred dollars," which is "exclusive of the £30 a year which I allow for my dear little Beulah's benefit; and exclusive of the interest of one third of the £1100 paid for the farm you reside upon." Lindley also quotes some comforting lines from the poet James Thomson.[19] (The Beulah mentioned was Susannah's daughter; the Murray and

109

Lindley clans, like many others, often named their children after family members.)

Lindley's letter to Susannah underlines how the Murrays invariably came together at a time of crisis to help family members who were in trouble. In particular, it shows Lindley's kindness towards his sisters. Even though he may not have had the warmest feelings towards her husband, he was steadfastly loyal and helpful to Susannah.

The rigors of farm life in upstate New York were no doubt a burden for Susannah, but she also suffered the death in 1807 of her son William Murray Willett, who was about 22 years old. A medical student, he died in the summer, indicating the likely cause was yellow fever, which decimated medical personnel and claimed many other lives in these years.[20] Susannah herself died a year later at the age of 45 after a slow, painful illness.

Susannah's death greatly affected Lindley and he devoted six pages in his *Memoirs* to it. Referring to the letters of relatives, Lindley says she "was so patient, so fully resigned to the will of God, so well prepared to leave the world, and to enter into a state of blessedness; that we have no cause to mourn."[21]

In his will, Robert Murray also treated his daughter Beulah with generosity. She received the corner lot to the north of Burnet's Key, certainly a valuable piece of property in maritime New York. In addition, she got a second lot at the corner of Broadway and Murray Street. (The name of this street bears no relation to the Robert Murray family.) Beulah may still have been single at the time of Robert's death, but by 1790 she had made what was perhaps the most successful marriage of the three Murray daughters. Her husband was Martin M. Hoffman, son of the well-known auctioneer Nicholas Hoffman. Nicholas Hoffman had been a member of the Committees of 51, 60 and 100, and became a loyalist. The two sons of Beulah and Martin became well-known figures in New York in the following generation—Judge Murray Hoffman and the merchant Lindley Murray Hoffman. Another relation was the Whig congressman

Josiah Ogden Hoffman, who represented Brooklyn and Staten Island from 1837–41.[22]

The eldest daughter of Robert Murray's family, Mary, was the least well treated of all the children. Robert left her £1,500, but she could not touch the money. It was to remain in the hands of her brother John, with only the interest going to her. Mary was also the sole child cut out in the distribution of the residue of the estate after all bequests had been fulfilled.[23]

Why this severe treatment of his daughter by Robert Murray? There were several sources of conflict. Mary's first marriage was made outside the Society of Friends and without her family's approval when she was only eighteen and Robert was away in England. The marriage caused her to be disowned by the Society of Friends. The groom was Ichabod Barnet, described in one account as "a young man of respectable connections, but gay and dissipated."[24] This is the same Ichabod Barnet who was running the Murray store in Elizabeth, New Jersey, at the time of the *Beulah* affair. He had first attempted to stonewall the Elizabeth investigating committee, but then implicated Robert and John.

The fact that Barnet was operating the store at all testifies that the Murrays had closed ranks and initially accepted the new husband. Mary's irregular marriage by itself would not seem the basis for Robert's slighting treatment of her—after all, Lindley himself had originally married outside Quaker discipline. But it is entirely possible that the outcome of the *Beulah* affair soured relations between Mary Barnet and Robert Murray. Even though the affair was his doing, Robert may have placed some blame on the Barnets for Lindley's forced exile.

The fact that Barnet died at the age of 28 lends credence to charges that he was "dissipated." After his death, Mary moved to Flushing, Long Island, where she met Edward Willet(t), second cousin of Gilbert Colden Willett. They wed, a marriage that lasted until his death about a decade later. There were no children. Though Mary may have displeased her father, there was no similar disposition among other members of the family. In his letters to his brother, Lindley often mentions his correspondence with her and sends her gifts such as calico dresses.

To his son John, Robert Murray bequeathed his wharf property, Robert's own house in Queen Street (where John was living), and property fronting on Water Street, which had to be among the most valuable lots in the city. The value of this inheritance is underlined by the fact that the will required John to pay the estate £4,000. Subsequent to Robert's death, John became the owner of the Grange, a country property adjoining Inclenberg, another indication that Robert's will enriched John.[25]

It is significant that among other bequests Robert left £200 for promoting the manumission of slaves and to support a free school for Negro children.[26] These were causes dear to the hearts of New York Quakers in general and John Junior in particular. John Junior was a founding incorporator and driving force of the New York Society for the Manumission of Slaves, ancestor of later abolition societies. Fellow members included Alexander Hamilton, John Jay, Isaac Collins and Uncle John Murray.

John Junior was equally committed to helping Native Americans, particularly the Oneida and other Indians of central New York state.[27] His feelings about these questions and other issues such as pacifism can be traced in 77 letters dated 1787–1806 written to James Bringhurst of Philadelphia, which are in the library of Swarthmore College.

An indication of the importance of John Junior in the American Quaker community was the fact that he accompanied the well-known British Friend Deborah Darby and her companion Rebecca Young as far south as Baltimore during their 1793 trip to America. John Junior described his adventures in a series of lively letters to his wife Catherine. Rebecca Young was evidently a caustic critic of the way things were done in America; obviously sharing a joke with his wife, John refers to her throughout the letters as "Rebukah."[28]

John Junior and his wife had three children, Mary (1784–1829), Robert (1786–1858) and Lindley (b. 1790). In

1806, Mary had fallen in love with a remarkable young man called Benjamin Perkins and wanted to marry him. It was a match that occasioned great anxiety on her parents' part, and with good reason. Benjamin was the son and associate of Dr. Elisha Perkins, whom one biographer has called "the apostle of one of those epochs of credulity which seize men from time to time." In other words, Elisha was a quack.[29]

The son of a respected New England physician, Elisha had also attained prominence as a doctor himself. Then, attracted by the theories of Galvani on the electrical properties of metals, he invented a device called "medical tractors." It consisted of a pair of metal bars used to stroke an affected area, supposedly drawing off noxious elements. The device caused great excitement among the public, and the treatment became known as Tractoration or Perkinism.

After Benjamin Perkins graduated from Yale in 1794, he had gone to London to promote his father's device, gaining support from some prominent Britons. In 1803, he established The Perkinean Institution, with Lord Rivers as its president and Sir William Barker as vice president. However, British physicians soon began questioning the method, and the satiric poem *Terrible Tractoration* by Christopher Caustic, M.D. (the American wit Thomas Green Fessenden) made it something of a laughing stock. (Bizarrely, Fessenden said later that Perkins had encouraged him to write the poem.) The debacle forced Benjamin to return to America.[30]

Benjamin's father has been described as being handsome and with a magnetic personality,[31] and his son obviously shared those qualities. Mary Murray was determined to have him. During the courtship, her father wrote Lindley asking if he knew anything about Benjamin's reputation. The quackery of Perkinism was not as evident at that time as it would appear later, and Benjamin was obviously talented at promotion. Everything about the young man, Lindley replied to John, "appeared to be very favourable." He also urged that John make appropriate financial arrangements with Perkins: "A liberal advance *now* may mean more to him and her, than twice the sum at a future period."[32] This money was needed to complete Perkins's payment to become a partner in the printing firm of Isaac Collins, who was Lindley Murray's publisher in New York. This arrangement with a future member of the Murray family was very much in Collins's interest. Lindley Murray was already a best-seller, and by far the most important name in the Collins stable.

In addition to letting his daughter have the man she wanted, John Junior perhaps had another idea in mind in setting up Perkins in business. Up to this point, Lindley's faithful younger brother had been handling all matters in the United States concerning the publication of Lindley's books. It was no easy task. The pace of printings in America had been accelerating. The first Lindley Murray textbook in the United States was the *English Reader*, issued in New York in 1799. Only a year later there were ten editions of Murray published in New York, Boston and Philadelphia, including the *Reader*, *Grammar*, an *Abridgement* of the grammar and the *Exercises*, an adjunct to the grammar. By the end of 1806, 67 editions of Murray's textbooks had been published in the United States in sixteen different cities. Such a burst of growth meant the job of being Lindley's American representative was arduous: printers had to be sought out and corresponded with; copies of new English editions had to be passed on to them; copies of American editions and reviews of the books had to be obtained, and sent back to Lindley in York.

In his exile, Lindley attached enormous importance to the broadcast of his works throughout his native land. In letter after letter to his brother John, Lindley made exacting demands for details about his books. Indeed, Lindley's concern had the aspect of a religious crusade. He was convinced he had a moral lesson to teach to the children of the new nation. As he wrote to John in 1801: "Thy kind and active exertions have already contributed greatly to circulate thy brother's labours for the benefit of the rising generation in America."[33]

The burden of helping the rising generation fell on John Junior. He must have been hard put to run his own business in New York, participate in the growing number of philanthropic activities in which he was involved, and still deal with the widening circle of printers publishing Lindley's books, not to mention catering to Lindley's voracious appetite for information about what was happening. And none of John's work was remunerated. Because there was no international copyright law, American printers did not pay any royalties for works originating in Britain. All the Murrays could hope to do was to pressure or cajole printers to issue works that were faithful copies of the carefully printed British originals.

In the spring of 1806, John's daughter Mary married Benjamin Perkins, and the new son-in-law undertook to share the task of dealing with Lindley's American publishers and keeping the exile informed about reviews of his books and other developments. The entry of Benjamin into the family is the most obvious reason why in the summer of 1806, a few months after the marriage, Lindley began to compose the autobiographical letters that became his *Memoirs*. Three decades had passed since the events of 1776, and Benjamin was new to the Murray clan. It is logical that he would have asked to be filled in on the events leading to Lindley's exile, to have background for promoting the books, dealing with printers and possibly suggesting Lindley for commendations.

According to Elizabeth Frank in her addendum to the *Memoirs*, the book was composed due to her suggestion. And twice in the *Memoirs* Lindley confirms this.[34] But based on the chronology, it is more likely that the *Memoirs* (or an earlier version) were originally composed to guide Benjamin Perkins. This would partially explain Lindley's reluctance to confront the facts of his conduct before the Revolution and his subsequent exile. Strong feelings about the Revolution were still widespread in America and Lindley did not want to endanger the prospects for his books or embarrass his family. If the autobiographical letters were composed for Elizabeth Frank alone (or for the British public), there would have been no reason to conceal his pre-Revolutionary activities and exile.

This analysis also explains, for example, why Lindley's reminiscences were cast in the form of letters. During part of this time, Elizabeth Frank lived with the Murrays; during the rest she lived a half-mile away and saw them constantly,[35] so letters would not really have been necessary. But if they had originally been mailed across the seas to Benjamin, the form seems more logical. These letters to Benjamin Perkins are not preserved, but in his correspondence with his brother, Lindley mentions (or assumes) on several occasions an exchange of missives with Perkins.[36]

For his part, Benjamin Perkins was happy to take on the responsibility of acting for this important author, and to keep him informed about reviews of his books and other developments. Lindley was pleased with the new arrangement and saw distinct advantages for the promotion of his books. Perkins, he wrote to John on April 1, 1806, after hearing from the young man, "is well qualified, in point of judgement, connexion, and disposition, to promote the credit and circulation of my books in America."

However, the Murrays' effort to control the printing of the books in the United States fell apart when Perkins suddenly died in New York on October 13, 1810.[37] It was a crushing blow. From this point on, Lindley seems gradually to have lost interest in pressuring his American printers to produce good-quality editions of his works, although he does make an effort to send to a few of the best-known printers corrected or enlarged versions of his works. Even this task grew difficult to accomplish— hundreds of separate editions of his textbooks were now coming off the presses in all parts of the nation.

When a person as young as Benjamin Perkins dies suddenly in this period, yellow fever is the likely cause. Carried by the mosquito *Aedes aegypti*, yellow fever had been a curse in New York since the early eighteenth century, but was at its worst between 1791 and 1821, when there was an outbreak nearly every year. Soon after Benjamin's death, John Junior and his family began to spend their summers in hilly Rockaway, New Jersey, fleeing (like many New York families) the city's miasmas. Since John Junior already had a country house, called The Grange, near Inclenberg, this summer departure may also be a barometer of the growing encroachment of the city on country estates. It certainly indicates that going to the countryside of mid-Manhattan was no protection from yellow fever.[38]

In 1819, Lindley's brother John, his ever-loyal ally, died in New York. He had been in Albany a few years before, visiting state officials on behalf of one of his good causes, when he took a heavy fall on the winter ice. He never fully recovered and from that point on, had been lame and suffered almost constant pain.[39] His death left Lindley as the sole surviving child of Robert and Mary Lindley Murray.

Quaker John's life, devoted to charity (and earning him the nickname "John Murray the Good"), was on the personal level quiet and restrained in the manner of the Friends. It contrasts markedly with the life lived by his more worldly Presbyterian uncle. From the moment on April 25, 1789, when he dressed himself in finery and accompanied John Broome and Theophylact Bache to present the official congratulations of the Chamber of Commerce to Gen. George Washington, newly arrived in New York for his Presidential inauguration, Presbyterian John had been immersed in the civic and cultural life of the city.[40]

A glimpse into the social life of Presbyterian John and his family can be found in a charming book called *A Season in New York: Letters of Harriet and Maria Trumbull*.[41] Harriet and Maria Trumbull, seventeen and fifteen respectively, were in New York for a season from their home in Lebanon, Connecticut, as paying guests in the home of the fashionable

117

Lady Kitty Duer, sister of Lord Stirling. Harriet and Maria were the daughters of Jonathan Trumbull, then governor of Connecticut, and granddaughters of Jonathan Trumbull, governor of Connecticut from 1769–1784. They were also nieces of the painter John Trumbull, who was a close friend of Presbyterian John Murray. (Presbyterian John, in fact, was well-known in the art circles of the time as a founder of the New York Academy of Fine Arts, which was to become the American Academy of Fine Arts.)[42]

In January 1801, Mary and Hannah Lindley Murray, Presbyterian John's daughters, called on the Trumbull girls to welcome them to the city. Soon after, the girls had tea and spent the evening with the Murrays at their city home. The Murrays were "charming people," Maria reported in a letter to her mother, "and treat us very affectionately—the young ladies [Mary and Hannah] are very accomplished. . . they live in a large house on Pearl Street—and are very rich."

Presbyterian John's wife, Hannah, a cousin of Mary Lindley Murray, had been born a Quaker. Maria Trumbull remarks that Hannah kept, in the style of the Friends, a house that was less ostentatious than her peers, but the family nevertheless entertained frequently. The children, however, followed John Murray's Presbyterian faith. The family attended the First Presbyterian Church in the city and the children were baptized there.

From this point on, the Trumbull girls saw the Murrays frequently and attended a ball given by the Murray daughters about a month later. In a letter of March 10, Harriet reiterates to her mother that the Murray daughters "are very amiable and accomplished. . . we saw a great many of their drawings and they play'd and sung for us."[43]

To say that Mary and Hannah Lindley Murray were accomplished is putting the case mildly. They would become internationally known for their book *The American Toilet* (1825), later reprinted as *The Toilet* (1867). This is an illustrated book of twenty rather syrupy riddles in the form of couplets. For instance, under the headline "A Wash to Smooth Wrinkles" is the following: "A daily portion of this essence use,/ Twill smooth the brow, and tranquil joy infuse." Between the headline and the couplet is a black-and-white lithograph of a crystal bowl with cover. The lithograph is printed with flaps so the reader can lift the cover of the bowl to find the solution of the riddle, in this case the word "Contentment." Similarly, the answer to the riddle "Use daily for your lips this precious dye:/They redden, and breathe the sweeter melody" is the word "Cheerfulness" concealed behind the cover of a cosmetics jar.

A preface to the 1867 edition, which has colored lithographs, explains the origin of the book:

> Many years ago, Miss Hannah and Miss Mary Murray, of New York, ladies of great wealth and culture, designed "The Toilet." They cut pictures from papers and pasted them on the leaves of little blank books, and the descriptions were in their own handwriting. It was originated and sold for charitable purposes, and the demand for it was so great that at length a thousand dollars was realized from the sale of it, and given to the Foreign Mission Society.[44]

On a more serious note, both young women were first-class linguists. They translated Torquato Tasso's epic poem *Jerusalem Delivered* from Italian, Ovid's "Fall of Phæton" from Latin, and from French a history of Hungary by Sacy and the sermons of Bishop Jean-Baptiste Massillon. In addition, they translated several operas from different languages. They also did original literary work, including a poem in eight books titled "Restoration of the Jews." Hannah also painted and wrote other verses and hymns.[45]

On Presbyterian John's death in 1808, apartments for Mary and Hannah were created at Inclenberg; they shared the old homestead with their sister Susan (wife of William

Ogden) and their brother, John R. Murray. Hannah Lindley Murray died in 1836. The year before, the grand old family house, built more than seven decades before by Robert Murray on his profits from the Seven Years' War, had been destroyed by fire.[46]

Lindley Murray: Finale

9

AFTER HE SETTLED IN HOLDGATE in 1785, Lindley Murray kept in constant touch with his relations in America. It was evidence of the close family bonds among the Murrays, but it was also a way of coping with the feeling of depression that had gripped him since his exile. What really began to lift his depression, though, was his emergence as a writer of books. One can sense it in his letters to his brother; increasingly, they are filled with publishing details, information on the progress of various editions in England and instructions concerning the broadcast of his works in America.

From his first book, *The Power of Religion* (1787), Lindley took a keen interest in the minutiae of publishing, particularly concerning revisions of his new editions. Such work, Lindley says in the *Memoirs*, "contributed to occupy some of my leisure hours; and, for a time, afforded a little amusement." Soon though, "it increased much beyond my expectation. . . My examination of the new editions, gave occasion to many corrections and considerable enlargements; which I flatter myself have improved the books."[1]

This concentrated activity continued for decades. To friends who worried that such hard work was not good for his health, he would say "It is better to wear away, than to rust away."[2] Occasionally, there were bouts of depression and illness, but his new work came as a kind of salvation. "In the course of my literary labours," he says, "I found that the mental exercise which accompanied them, was not a little beneficial to my health. The motives which excited me to write, and the objects which I hoped to accomplish, were of a nature calculated to cheer the mind and to give the animal spirits a salutary impulse. I am persuaded that if I had suffered my time to pass away, with little or no employment, my health would have been still more impaired, my spirits depressed, and perhaps my life considerably shortened."[3]

Lindley always showed particular interest in reviews—he wanted to know how his contemporaries were receiving his works and was quick to exploit favorable comments by asking printers to insert them in the endpages of his books. Lindley's success, of course, immediately made him a target of his competitors. We have seen how Lyman Cobb complained in America. As editions of Lindley's various works issued from the press, he added corrections and emendations based on criticisms. He also began to take an interest in what his competitors were doing in their books. Frequently, he asked John Murray, Junior, to send him the works of competitors.[4]

In America Lindley's main competitor was Noah Webster, who had something of a tangled relationship with the Murray family. In 1787, a few years after Lindley's departure for Britain, Webster had arrived in New York to edit the *American Magazine*, but the venture failed within the year. However, Webster was back in New York in 1793 to take on the editorship of a newspaper, the daily *Minerva*, intended to advocate the Federalist party line in the city. Webster had probably encountered the Murrays during his first stint in the city, but he certainly would have come in contact with John Murray, Junior, during his second stay. Webster entertained frequently, and John was a member of the Federalist camp in New York.

The *Minerva* venture did not go well, however, and on April 1, 1798, Webster withdrew from active editorship. His finances were in disarray. On December 1, 1800, Lindley wrote to John: "I hope my Brother will invest in the New York Bank, what ever money of mine he may have recd. from N Webster's Bond."[5] From the chronology, it seems that the Webster loan probably dated from his withdrawal from New York, and was arranged by John Murray, Junior, using Lindley's money. From the Murrays' point of view, it could not hurt to have the leading American text-book writer literally in their debt just as Lindley's own works were beginning to appear on the American market.[6]

The income from Webster's textbooks was a likely source of surety for the bond. Lindley was well aware of Webster's impor-tance in the textbook field. In a letter of September 5, 1803, Lindley asked John to send the latest edition of Webster's gram-mar and sent Webster a copy of his own grammar. Within a few years, Murray's *Grammar* and the *English Reader* had almost fully replaced Webster's competing titles. Only Webster's speller con-tinued as a best seller.[7]

If the Murrays thought they were buying Webster's approba-tion with their loan, they were much mistaken. Murray's ascen-dancy did not please the prickly Webster. In the preface to his 1807 *A Philosophical and Practical Grammar of the English Language*, his attempt to counter Murray, Webster attacked Murray's grammar for stealing from his own.[8] He continued his attacks over the next several years following the publication of Murray's large-format two-volume *Grammar*, a book in which Murray tried to answer all the objections that had been raised about his *Grammar*.

In 1815, John Murray, Junior, sent along a copy of the latest Webster effusion. Perhaps sensitive to John's previous relation-ship with Webster, Lindley replied at length. "Noah Webster," he says, "is not correct in saying that I have made '*numerous* extracts from his Grammar.' I have looked over and reckoned them; and I believe that *exclusive* of the one to which I have put his name, as it was a long one, and to which he does not object, they do not, when put together, amount to *two pages* of the American Octavo Grammar, which contain more than *Six hundred pages*." However, Lindley sent along a note to be inserted in the next

Collins edition of the large-format *Grammar*, so as "to remove every shadow of objection."[9]

In addition to his continual production of, and then revision of his books, Lindley kept a close eye on what was happening in the world around him. In 1814, Hannah Richardson succeeded Elizabeth Frank in the Murray household and remained as a housekeeper-companion until the death of his widow in 1834. When she went to town to shop, Hannah Richardson could never chat for long with friends because the invalid Lindley almost counted the minutes until her return with his letters, his daily paper, his weekly *Newcastle Chronicle,* and the news of his acquaintances. Though he would not allow a newspaper into the house on Sundays, Lindley made sure he did not miss any news by reading two papers on Monday.[10]

Although he followed the news closely, events in France that significantly altered the intellectual climate in Britain—leading, for example, to Burke's *Reflections on the Revolution in France*, the newspaper *The Anti-Jacobin* and the magazine *Anti-Jacobin Review*—never seemed to affect Lindley's basic Enlightenment outlook. Lindley was able to keep the faith with his reading of Scottish Enlightenment writers such as Hugh Blair. But given the climate in England, it is notable that he never, in his correspondence with John, said a word against the revolutionaries of France. A few years later, however, he expressed disdain for Napoleon. It was as if Lindley refused to oppose the French Revolution as long as it was moving towards overthrow of the monarchy and struggling towards establishing a post-revolutionary order. But once the despotism of Napoleon became evident, Lindley opposed him.[11]

This is certainly not to say that Lindley was in any way a revolutionary. Another aspect of embracing the Scottish Enlightenment was the lure of its respectability, morally as well as intellectually. Lindley frequently refers to his desire to inculcate his readers with "piety and virtue" and "sound morality" and to safeguard them from "everything that might stain the delicacy of their minds."[12] Such statements should be seen in the context of the times and the charges of immorality that were flung at the French revolutionaries. But Lindley's refusal to specifically attack the French Revolution, which would have been so easy to do, reveals something significant about his attitude.

By 1794, Lindley had been in exile for a decade. In the spring of that year, he had begun writing his grammar, the literary project that would launch his textbook career. His mood was buoyant. Soon after, John Jay, his former fellow student in the office of Benjamin Kissam, came to England to negotiate issues arising out of the Treaty of Paris that had ended the Revolution. On July 15, Lindley wrote to Jay, sending along a copy of *The Power of Religion*, and expressing his confidence that Jay would bring about "a speedy and happy dispersion of those clouds of hostility which have been some time gathering, and which seemed of late ready to involve the two countries in confusion and distress." He also invited Jay to visit Holdgate: "It would be a peculiar gratification if the course of thy travels should include York, to have the favour of seeing thee and enjoying thy company at my house."[13]

On August 22, Jay replied from the Royal Hotel, Pall Mall, London, saying of the proposed visit: "I dare not promise that satisfaction, being so much and so constantly under the direction of circumstances I cannot control." But Jay, who was so deeply involved on the patriot side in the *Beulah* affair, goes on to register what can only be interpreted as his brutally frank appraisal of Lindley's past actions: "The sentiments diffused throughout your book are just, striking and useful; but, my good friend, our opinions are oftener right than our conduct. Among the strange things of this world, nothing seems more strange than that men pursuing happiness should knowingly quit the right and take the wrong road, and frequently do what their judgements neither approve nor prefer. Yet so is the fact."[14]

Here, Jay is expressing his amazement that Lindley, a person "on the right road," that is, one whose sentiments should have led him into the patriot camp, took a course of action in the Committee of 100, and possibly afterwards, that he fully knew was dead wrong. It is a damning, heartbreaking verdict from a person of consequence whom Lindley was soliciting for friendship and possibly for future aid in returning to New York. Jay's reply shattered Lindley's hopes of ending his exile at that time.

Jay goes on to say that "only one adequate plan has ever appeared in the world" for dealing with "moral and physical evil," and "that is the Christian dispensation. . . I mention these things that you may see the state of my mind relative to these interesting subjects, and to relieve yours from doubts which your friendship for me might render disagreeable."[15] After dashing his hopes, Jay tells Lindley that though he had done wrong at the time of the Revolution, he, as a Christian, forgives him. It was a meaningful theme for a sincere Quaker like Lindley, but it must have been cold comfort.

The tone of Lindley's July 15 letter to Jay had been positive and hopeful, but Jay's stern verdict threw Lindley into a deep depression and illness. Work on the grammar stopped.[16] As usual in times of great stress, his health suffered, and he began to contemplate, or even wish for, death. "At the close of the year 1794," says Lindley, describing the period in the *Memoirs*, "I was seized with a severe illness, which continued for many weeks; and reduced me to so feeble a state, that my recovery was very much doubted. During the continuance of this affliction I was often desirous, that, if it were the will of Divine Providence, I might be removed from this state of trouble and be landed safely. . . on those happy shores where there is neither sickness nor sorrow."[17] Only the completion of his *Grammar* and its immediate success rescued Lindley from this deep depression.

Though he had crushed Lindley's hopes in 1794, John Jay worked closely with John Murray, Junior, on the New York Society for the Manumission of Slaves. In 1821, Jay wrote to Lindley with condolences on the death of John Junior. Jay's attitude towards Lindley had changed. For one thing, Lindley was now an internationally famous writer, approaching the stature of Jay himself. The passions, if not the lessons, of the Revolution had faded. It was also a case of an old man closing the book on former enmities. Referring to their mutual health problems, Jay wrote: "We have both passed the usual term of human life or (as the lawyers say) our leases have expired, and we are holding over. Your affectionate friend, John Jay."[18] This conciliatory gesture heartened Lindley and he reciprocated it. He added praise of Jay to his 1823 revision of the *Memoirs*.[19]

Even before his 1794 crisis, however, Lindley had been doing his work despite considerable physical disability, which he discusses with hypochondriacal frequency and sometimes at length in the *Memoirs* and his letters to John Junior and others. Since Lindley used the excuse of health to explain matters such as his departure from New York after the British evacuation and his exile to Britain, one tends to take other references to health—other than his obvious depressions—with a grain of salt.

But there can be little doubt that after Lindley reached the age of 40, he began to suffer from some debilitating illness. As early as 1785, he tells his father he cannot walk across his living room more than ten or twelve times without feeling weak for the rest of the day. For the remainder of his life, he constantly complained of colds, flu, or arthritis. The possibility exists that he could have contracted a case of multiple sclerosis or muscular dystrophy, which often appear about age 40. But he lived until the age of 81, had a healthy, ruddy countenance, worked long hours on his books, had the dexterity to conduct a wide correspondence in a firm clear hand, had an excellent memory and was favored with excellent vision—even in his last years he could read fine print, though with the aid of spectacles.[20] These facts argue against multiple sclerosis or muscular dystrophy as a cause of Lindley's health problems. A possible combination of causes may lie in arthritis of the spine exacerbated by frequent cases of the flu.

From 1809 on, Lindley was unable to go out in his carriage or even spend time in a chair in the garden. Even light exercise caused muscular weakness. The house at Holdgate was drafty and the fire had to be lit every day, even in summer. In 1810, he discharged a small stone. He spent the last sixteen years of his life confined to his house, moving about his room in an armchair equipped with wheels, which is today preserved in York.[21] But despite these disabilities, Lindley was never fully and finally confined to his bed until his last illness.

On January 10, 1826, while at dinner, he had a "paralytic affection" in his left hand, probably a small stroke since it was of short duration.[22] In the Quaker Collection at the Library of Haverford College is a copy of a letter from Lindley to the Quaker evangelical, Joseph John Gurney. Dated February 1, 1826, it is the last letter we have, although Elizabeth Frank said he was writing until three days before his death.[23]

On February 13, there was a return of numbness in the hand, but it subsided. In the evening, Lindley had an acute pain in the groin, accompanied by violent sickness. During the night, he had a long spell of unconsciousness. About 7:00 A.M. the morning of February 16, the severe pain in his groin returned, forcing him to cry out. Hannah came to his side and he spoke to her "in the most tenderly, affectionate manner." He died at 8:30 A.M.[24]

On February 22, Lindley Murray was interred at the Friends' Burying Ground at Bishophill in York, where the famed American Quaker missionary and anti-slavery crusader John Woolman had been buried 50 years earlier.[25] Elizabeth Frank was part of the large assemblage that followed him to his grave, but his beloved and stalwart Hannah, his wife of 58 years, was too overcome to attend the burial.[26]

In his will, dated February 1, 1821, Lindley left his money to provide for his wife while she lived. He bequeathed books to various friends, including those he had used for many of his selections in the *English Reader*, the *Introduction* and the *Sequel*. Five volumes of Blair's *Sermons* from his library went to his York friend Samuel Tuke, in trust for his son William Murray Tuke. To Hannah Richardson he gave the six volumes of Doddridge's *Family Expositor* and Bishop Horne's *Commentary on the Psalms*. Elizabeth Frank received books and was given charge of his papers and letters, which pursuant to his instructions, she destroyed.[27]

Attended by Hannah Richardson, Hannah Dobson Murray lived until 1834. After her death, Lindley's other bequests were distributed, and the remaining $30,500 was bequeathed to set up a fund in New York. Its annual income was to be used "in liberating black people who may be held in slavery, assisting them when freed, and giving their descendants, or the descendants of other black persons, suitable education; in promoting the civilization and instruction of the Indians of North America; and in the purchase and distribution of books tending to promote piety and virtue, and the truth of Christianity." Among those books, *The Power of Religion*—"with the author's latest corrections and improvements"—"may form a considerable part." The New York fund still operates today.[28]

The most judicious judgement on Lindley Murray's mind and attitudes is that of Elizabeth Frank:

> He was a true patriot. America, his native land, the abode of his relations, and his own during a great part of his life, was dear to him: England was also dear to him; it was his adopted country, and the scene of his greatest usefulness. He rejoiced in the prosperity of both countries; and particularly wished that peace and amity should prevail between them. He was a friend of liberty, both civil and religious; a warm asserter of the just rights of man, and averse to despotic power, whether lodged in the hands of one, or of many; but at the same time, he was a friend of order, a strenuous supporter of good government, and opposed to all wild theories and useless innovation."[29]

And of his writings, she adds with equal justice: "His works have produced much practical good to society. And this character certainly entitles them to a respectable rank in the republic of letters."[30]

Appendix
Lindley Murray's Publishing Numbers

United States

The most painstaking analysis of the printing numbers for a large-circulation textbook in this era is that of E. Jennifer Monaghan in *A Common Heritage: Noah Webster's Blue-back Speller*. Examining Webster's account books, Monaghan establishes a minimum of 10,650,000 copies of the speller in the years from 1804 to Webster's death in 1843.[1]

For the same years, 1804–1843, Webster's bibliographer, Emily Skeel, lists 304 American editions (i.e., printings) of the Webster speller. That would mean an average edition of perhaps 35,000 copies. Skeel casts a wide net, counting editions for which there is any possible evidence, including advertisements. There is no question that all copies of many editions of early textbooks have been lost, so her reckoning is fair enough, and is valuable for establishing the size of an average edition of a Webster speller.[2]

To extrapolate from Monaghan's Webster numbers to reach some conclusion about Murray's numbers, however, we must use a single bibliography that contains information about both authors. The volumes of *American Bibliography* are the best available tool.[3]

From 1801 through 1840, *American Bibliography* lists 221 editions of Webster literacy textbooks (174 editions of his speller and 47 of his grammars and readers). For the same years, it lists 925 editions of Murray literacy textbooks (including 342 editions of the *English Reader*).

If one were to use the figure of 35,000 copies per edition for the 925 editions of Murray from 1801–1839, that total would come to over 32 million copies. However, to accept such an estimate would be unwise. The figure of 35,000 applies to sales of a speller. This was the book that taught children to read; a reader was a more advanced book, for children who already knew how to read. Until readers were published in a series, from easy to more advanced, the speller held a place similar to that of the first book in a basal reading series of today.

In addition, Webster kept a tight rein on licenses for his textbooks; so when a printer bought the rights, a large run of each edition was likely. There was also a difference in marketing. Webster's speller had become a commodity, a family necessity available in almost every general store after 1830 or so. The readers and grammars that formed the bulk of Murray's output would probably have to be purchased from a book store, and so may have been less widely distributed.

While the lion's share of Webster editions were of his speller, Lindley Murray was selling a wider range of texts. They were, in order of publication: the *English Grammar*, the *English Exercises* and the *Key to the Exercises* (both adjuncts to the *Grammar*), the *Abridgement* of the grammar (intended for younger students), the *English Reader*, the *Sequel to the English Reader*, the *Introduction to the English Reader*, the *Lecteur François* and *Introduction au Lecteur François* (his two French-language texts), *An English Spelling-Book* and his *First Book for Children*.

Hard facts on the exact numbers of books printed per edition are thin on the ground, but there is one intriguing piece of evidence from the British printings of Murray. It comes from Murray's secretary, Elizabeth Frank, in her addendum to the *Memoirs*, published in 1826. Frank undoubtedly handled correspondence with Murray's printers and was therefore in a good position to know exact publishing figures. "For many years past," she says, "every edition of the Grammar has consisted of ten thousand copies; of the Exercises, ten thousand; of the Key, six thousand; Abridgement of the Grammar, twelve thousand; of the Spelling Book, and of the First Book for Children, ten thousand. Each edition of the English Reader and of the Introduction to the English Reader, consist of ten thousand copies; of the Sequel to the English Reader, six thousand; of the Lecteur François, and the Introduction au Lecteur François, each three thousand."[4]

There is some corroboration for similar sorts of numbers in the United States, at least for two of the titles. In a "notice" in the front of the *Sequel to the English Reader*, published in New York in 1808, Collins & Perkins stated that in the ten years of its publication, there had been about 25 editions of the *Grammar*, with annual sales of 35,000 copies (a total of about 350,000). For the eight years in which the *Abridgement* had been published, it had sold 50,000 copies a year (or 400,000) in 40 editions. That averages 14,000 copies per edition of the *Grammar* and 10,000 copies per edition of the *Abridgement*.[5]

(The Collins & Perkins numbers, by the way, apply only to editions that they controlled, or as they put it, those that came "in *purity*, from the pen of the author." They did not include non-approved editions published in Boston, Philadelphia, Worcester and Hartford.)

The number of copies in each edition must have expanded in the years that followed. By 1813, the *English Reader* was being stereotyped by Collins in New York, possibly the first large-run stereotyped book; by the mid-1820s, leading printers had more powerful presses. In 1829, a Collins "advertisement" notes that six of eleven listed Murray textbooks are stereotyped. All printers realized considerable savings per copy from larger runs; stereotyping and faster presses made larger editions easier to produce.

Some educated guesses are necessary to estimate total numbers for Murray. Let's leave out of the equation the two French books, the spelling book and the *First Book for Children*—they amount only to seventeen editions from 1801 through 1840. Equally, let's leave out the copies sold before 1801 and the editions after 1840 when Murray's sales were in decline.

Based on the slender evidence and wishing to make a conservative estimate, I feel that in the 1801–1840 span an average run of 10,000 copies per edition can be applied to the less well-known of Murray's texts—the *English Exercises,* the *Key to the Exercises* and the *Introduction* and *Sequel to the English Reader.* They amount to 251 titles, which can be rounded off to 2.5 million copies.

For the 657 editions of his major books—the *English Reader,* the *Grammar* and the *Abridgement*—a conservative estimate would be 15,000 copies per edition over the four decades. (After all, the *Grammar* had reached 14,000 in its first decade.) That would be 9,855,000 copies, or a round figure of 10 million. The combined figures come to 12.5 million literacy textbooks written by Murray and sold in the first four decades of the nineteenth century in the United States.

The *English Reader* alone has 342 editions in the 1801–1840 list. With an average edition of 15,000, its total would come to 5,130,000. It does not seem out of place to round off the *English Reader* total to 5 million copies. Using the above educated guess of 10,000 copies for each edition for the 153 editions of the *Introduction to the English Reader* and the *Sequel to the English Reader,* and adding the figures for the *English Reader,* we get a total of about 6.5 million copies of the three-reader sequence in the first four decades of the century. All the readers have the same Scottish Enlightenment-style content.

The *American Bibliography* figures for 1801–1840 for Noah Webster's speller in the United States should come very close to the 10,650,000 established by E. Jennifer Monaghan for the 1804–1843 period. In fact, because the *American Bibliography* lists only 174 of the 304 editions of spellers documented by Skeel, the former would total about 6 million copies of the speller (estimating 35,000 per edition). The 47 editions of other literacy-related Webster textbooks listed in the *American Bibliography*—grammars and readers—had much smaller editions, averaging about 3,000 each, or some 140,000 copies. Even if we use the much larger numbers for the spellers in Skeel, the highest Webster total for literacy-related textbooks (excluding school dictionaries) for the first four decades of the nineteenth century is some 10,850,000 copies.[6]

Under this reckoning—if the estimated sizes of Murray editions are correct—Murray emerges as the most widely-sold author of literacy textbooks in the United States, in the first four decades of the century. None of the rivals to Murray or Webster was even close, as will be indicated below.

Britain

The bibliographer Joseph Smith lists the following editions of Murray's texts in Britain:

> *English Grammar* (1795): 52 editions to 1832.
> *English Exercises, Adapted to the Grammar:* (1797) 56 to 1854.
> *Key to the Exercises* (1797) 25 to 1839.
> *An Abridgement of L. Murray's English Grammar* (1801): 133 to 1845.
> *English Reader* (1799): 25 to 1842.
> *Sequel to the English Reader* (1800): 8 to 1843.
> *Introduction to the English Reader* (1801): 31 to 1836.
> *Lecteur François* (1802): 6 to 1824.
> *Introduction au Lecteur François* (1802): 31 to 1836.
> *An English Spelling-Book* (1804): 44 to 1834.
> *First Book for Children* (1805): 23 to 1859.
> Two-volume *Grammar* (including *Exercises* and *Key*) (1808): 7 to 1834.[7]

Therefore, editions of Murray textbooks total 441. His two-volume *Grammar*, which included the *Exercises* and the *Key,* was printed in seven editions from 1808 through 1834. I have not included it in my calculations because it was more a reference book than a schoolbook, seen by Murray as a vehicle for answering the considerable objections that had been raised about his

Grammar, largely by rivals. In addition, Smith lists 49 editions of nine other Murray titles.

Once again, the most important source for estimating the size of printings of Murray's textbooks in Britain is the testimony of Elizabeth Frank quoted above. Multiplying Frank's figures by the number of editions listed by Smith, we get a total of 4,215,000. There could have been smaller runs earlier and later in Murray's career. But a figure of 3 million Murray books produced in Britain in the first four decades of the century seems a rock-bottom minimum. A total of 4 million Murray books of all sorts eventually sold in Britain seems a sound and conservative estimate.

Totals

Webster had no significant sales in Britain. The 12.5 million copies of Murray produced in the United States plus the 3 million in Britain during the first four decades of the century gives Murray a total of 15.5 million, making him the largest-selling author in the world in the first four decades of the nineteenth century. The Bible, of course, was the largest-selling book.

The rapidly expanding school system in America made it unique in terms of textbook sales; they were matched nowhere else. Other works of fiction and nonfiction paled in comparison in terms of sales. In these years, school textbook production of a substantial dimension did not exist except in the United States, Britain and a few countries of western Europe. Elsewhere, schooling was confined to a narrow elite.

Dominance in the United States

While the total figures for Murray must necessarily be approximate, what is indisputable is how dominant the *English Reader* was in the United States as a reading text in the years 1815 through 1836. Below is a listing of the number of editions listed for the *English Reader* from its first American appearance in 1799 through 1860. The numbers through 1844 are from *American Bibliography*. The rest are from the National Union Catalogue.

Number of Editions of the *English Reader* from its First American Appearance in 1799 through 1860

Year	Editions	Year	Editions	Year	Editions	Year	Editions
1799	3	1815	16	1837	6	1850	0
1800	3	1816	10	1838	5	1851	1
1801	1	1817	12	1839	4	1852	2
1802	1	1818	6	1840	6	1853	2
1803	4	1819	17	1841	5	1854	0
1804	2	1820	12	1842	4	1855	0
1805	5	1821	11	1843	5	1856	1
1806	4	1822	6	1844	3	1857	0
1807	1	1823	14	1845	4	1858	0
1808	4	1824	13	1846	4	1859	0
1809	5	1825	19	1847	3	1860	0
1810	8	1826	20	1848	1	1860	0
1811	5	1827	13	1849	1	**Total**	**6**
1812	6	1828	13	**Total**	**51**		
1813	8	1829	13				
1814	8	1830	8				
Total	**68**	1831	7				
		1832	10				
		1833	8				
		1834	6				
		1835	12				
		1836	13				
		Total	**259**				

The reasons why the number of editions of the *English Reader* begins to ease in 1837 is clear enough. The financial panic of that year may have had something to do with it, but a serious new rival had appeared on the scene. William Holmes McGuffey's *Eclectic*

Readers series had begun publication in 1836 and was an immediate success. The books in the series were much more child-oriented than the *English Reader*, with simpler language, larger type and illustrations (reflecting a changing, more sympathetic view of the child). Over the next decade, the McGuffey series almost entirely replaced the Murray readers. By 1850, 7 million McGuffeys had been sold, and Murray had all but disappeared.

The *McGuffey Readers* went on to dominate the market in the second half of the nineteenth century, eventually selling some 122 million individual copies, the largest number of textbooks ever sold under the name of a single author. Another reading series, that of Samuel Worcester, also ate into Murray's dominance. (Worcester sued McGuffey for plagiarism in 1838: the suit was settled out of court.)[8]

The reason why the number of Murray's *English Readers* leaped in 1815 probably had to do with the end of the War of 1812. Pent-up demand apparently caused the leap to sixteen editions in 1815, a figure not matched until 1819.

From 1815 through 1836, Murray crushed all rivals. Webster's reader, hardly serious competition after 1805, breathed its last in 1816. Starting in 1812, editions of the *English Reader* surpassed the combined totals of the *American Preceptor* and the *Columbian Orator*, both written by Murray's closest rival of the time, Caleb Bingham. After that, the gap continually widened. New rivals appeared on the scene in the 1820s, but they were no match for the *English Reader*. In 1824, all four of Murray's chief rivals—Bingham, Lyman Cobb, Albert Picket and John Pierpont—produced in combination less than half as many editions of their readers as the *English Reader* alone. It was a pattern that basically continued through 1836.

By 1827, Murray, chiefly because of the *English Reader*, was so essential a part of the fabric of American life that one commentator called him "the immortal Murray." It proved to be a gossamer immortality.

Notes

I have used the following abbreviations:

LM—Lindley Murray

JM—John Murray, brother of Lindley Murray

FHLS—Friends' Historical Library at Swarthmore College

NYHS—New-York Historical Society

NYPL—New York Public Library

NYMFS—New York Meeting for Sufferings, Society of Friends

Chapter 1. On the Trail of the Murrays

[1] Christopher J. Schuberth, *The Geology of New York City and Environs* (Garden City, N.Y., 1968), 1–13; "Old New York," *Evening Post*, Dec. 10, 1873, reprinted in *The Bowne Family of Flushing, L.I.,* compiled by Edith King Wilson (New York, 1948), 95–105.

[2] Jeremiah Goodrich, in his edition of Lindley Murray, *English Reader* (Providence, 1837), preface.

[3] Ingrid Tieken-Boon van Ostade, ed., *Two Hundred Years of Lindley Murray* (Münster, Germany, 1996); David A. Reibel, ed., *Lindley Murray (1745–1826): The Educational Works* (London: Routledge/Thoemmes Press, 1996).

[4] E. Jennifer Monaghan, *A Common Heritage: Noah Webster's Blue-Back Speller* (Hamden, Conn., 1983).

[5] Lindley Murray, *Memoirs of the Life and Writings of Lindley Murray: In a Series of Letters Written by Himself. With a Preface and Continuation of the Memoirs, by Elizabeth Frank* (York, England, 1826); Stephen Allott, *Lindley Murray 1745–1826: Quaker Grammarian* (York, England, 1991).

[6] Murray, *Memoirs*, v–vii, 1–2, 133, hereafter cited as *Memoirs*.

[7] *Memoirs*, 43.

[8] Lorenzo Sabine, *Biographical Sketches of Loyalists of the American Revolution* (1864; rpt. Port Washington, N.Y., 1966), 2: 112–15, 560.

[9] William Henry Egle, *Pennsylvania Genealogies* (Harrisburg, Pa., 1896), 526–40. Another historian who saw through Lindley's tale was Oscar T. Barck, Jr., *New York City During the War for Independence* (New York, 1931).

[10] John M. Lindly, *The History of the Lindley-Lindsley-Linsley Families in America* (Winfield, Iowa, 1924), 343.

Chapter 2. The Murrays and Lindleys of Pennsylvania

[1] *Memoirs*, 3; George R. Beyer, ed., *Guide to the Historical Markers of Pennsylvania* (Harrisburg, 1991), 71.

[2] Sarah Murray, *In the Olden Time: A Short History of the Descendants of John Murray the Good* (New York, 1894), 2; Lindly, *Lindley-Lindsley-Linsley Families*, 317–40; Milam Myrl Ewing, *Jacob Marion Lindley: His Ancestors and Descendants: A Genealogy* (Tulsa, Okla., 1978), 7–8.

[3] Frederick B. Tolles, *Meeting House and Counting House: The Quaker Merchants of Colonial Philadelphia* (New York, 1948), 98–9, 100 n. 35; Arthur Cecil Bining, *Pennsylvania Iron Manufacture in the Eighteenth Century* (1938; rpt., Harrisburg, 1987), 34 ff.

[4] Alan Tully, *William Penn's Legacy: Politics and Structure in Provincial Pennsylvania, 1726–1755* (Baltimore, 1977), 20, 32, 85–6, 95, 227 n. 33; James G. Leyburn, *The Scotch-Irish: A Social History* (Chapel Hill, N.C., 1962), 191; Albert Cook Myers, *Immigration of Irish Quakers Into Pennsylvania* (Swarthmore, Pa., 1902), 306; Lindly, *Lindley-Lindsey-Linsley Families*, 317–18.

[5] Lindly, *Lindley–Lindsey–Linsley Families*, 323.

[6] *Memoirs*, 5.

[7] Tully, *William Penn's Legacy*, 177–80.

[8] *Memoirs*, 3; Sarah Murray, *In Olden Time*, 2.

[9] Arthur L. Jensen, *Maritime Commerce of Colonial Pennsylvania* (Madison, Wisc., 1967), 89.

Chapter 3. The Spectacular Rise of Robert Murray in New York

[1] *Memoirs*, 8–9; Egle, *Pennsylvania Genealogies*, 527; population statistics from Lawrence A. Cremin, *American Education: The Colonial Experience, 1607–1783* (New York, 1970), 571–2; Thomas Bender, *New York Intellect* (New York, 1987), 11.

[2] Virginia D. Harrington, *The New York Merchant on the Eve of the Revolution* (1935; rpt. Gloucester, Mass., 1964), 11–46, 148. Among other old–money families were the Verplancks, DePeysters, Barclays, Lispenards, Van Horns, Ludlows, Gouverneurs, Duycknicks, Clarksons and Brinckerhofs; also among those prominent in colonial commerce were the Franks, Levy, Seixas, Isaacs, Gomez, Hendricks, Hays, Myers, Judah, Pinto and Lopez families, part of the city's vibrant Jewish community.

[3] Hugh Barbour and J. William Frost, *The Quakers* (New York, 1988), 86; Harrington, *New York Merchant*, 52, 153.

[4] Harrington, *New York Merchant*, 354; Kenneth Jackson, ed., *Encyclopedia of New York City* (New Haven, 1995), 361.

[5] Thomas C. Cochran, "An Analytical View of Early American Business and Industry," in Joseph R. Frese, S.J., and Jacob Judd, eds., *Business Enterprise in Early New York* (Tarrytown, N.Y., 1979), 5.

[6] Harrington, *New York Merchant*, 52; *New York Mercury*, April 18, 1768; Holt's *New York Journal*, April 21, 1768.

[7] "Plan of New York Surveyed in 1766 and 1767 by Bernard Ratzer," in John A. Stevens, Jr., *Colonial Records of the New York Chamber of Commerce* (New York, 1867), unpaginated insert before p. 397; I. N. Phelps Stokes, *The Iconography of Manhattan Island 1498–1909* (New York, 1922), 4: 767.

[8] On insurance, Harrington, *New York Merchant*, 155; on indigo, letter in Joshua Delaplaine Papers, NYHS, Misc. Microfilm Reel 10b.

[9] On Murray & Pearsall store, Weyman's *New York Gazette*, June 25, 1759, and numerous subsequent advertisements; Wilson, *Bowne Family of Flushing*, 11–13.

[10] Harrington, *New York Merchant*, 333–6.

[11] For example, Joseph A. Scoville (writing as Walter Barrett), *The Old Merchants of New York City* (New York, 1885), 1: 289; also Robert Murray biography in the *American Cyclopedia of Biography*.

[12] Harrington, *New York Merchant*, 50–52.

[13] Joshua Delaplaine Papers, NYHS, Misc. Microfilm, Reel 26.

[14] Minutes, New York Meeting for Sufferings, 1:11, FHLS.

[15] Carl Bridenbaugh, *Cities in Revolt: Urban Life in America, 1743–1776* (1955; rpt. New York, 1971), 339.

[16] Maud Wilder Goodwin et al., eds., *Historic New York* (New York, 1897), 317; John J. Gallagher, *The Battle of Brooklyn, 1776* (New York, 1995), 161.

[17] Sarah Murray, *In Olden Time*, 4–5.

[18] Robert Murray biography in *Dictionary of American Biography* (New York, 1934), 7: 365; *Scribner's Monthly*, February 1876, 466; *In Olden Time*, 8.

[19] Tolles, *Meeting House and Counting House*, 82; see letters between Lindley Murray and the Pemberton Family in Lindley Murray Papers at the Library of Swarthmore College and at the New-York Historical Society.

[20] Tolles, *Meeting House and Counting House*, 82.

[21] Murray, *In Olden Time*, 5; Alice Colden Wadsworth, "Sketch of the Colden and Murray Families," 1819 MS., Ford Collection, NYPL, 29.

[22] Bender, *New York Intellect*, 37, 38.

Chapter 4. The Enlightenment Education of Lindley Murray

[1] *Memoirs*, 8.

[2] Cremin, *American Education*, 402.

[3] *Memoirs*, 8.

[4] *Memoirs*, 9–10.

[5] Allott, *Lindley Murray*, 34, n. 8; Cremin, *American Education*, 402.

[6] *Memoirs*, 15–16.

[7] Allott, *Lindley Murray*, 35 n. 11.

[8] Charles Roberts Autograph Collection, Haverford College Library.

[9] *Memoirs*, 16–19.

[10] *Memoirs*, 20–24.

[11] *Memoirs*, 31; see also Bender, *New York Intellect*, 11–12.

[12] Letter of Peter Jay to John Jay, in Richard Morris, ed., *John Jay: Making of a Revolutionary: Unpublished Papers 1745-1780* (New York, 1975), 51–52; also 52 n. 2.

[13] *Memoirs*, 33; Bender, *New York Intellect*, 11; instances of Lindley's legal advice to the family are scattered throughout his letters at the Library of Swarthmore College.

[14] Quoted in Frank Monaghan, *John Jay: Defender of Liberty* (New York, 1935), 33.

[15] Morris, *John Jay: Making of a Revolutionary*, 67; *Memoirs*, 33.

[16] Monaghan, *John Jay*, 39.

[17] Morris, *John Jay: Making of a Revolutionary*, 92–94.

[18] *Memoirs*, 8; Anthony Michael Ramsay, *The Travels of Cyrus* (London, 1752); G. D. Henderson, *Chevalier Ramsay* (London, 1952), vii, 109, 114, 117–18, 207, 215, 226; Julia Nash Murphy, "Schools and Schooling in Eighteenth Century Philadelphia," (Ph.D. diss., Bryn Mawr, 1970), 205–6.

[19] *Memoirs*, 4, 16.

[20] Andrew Hook, "Philadelphia, Edinburgh and the Scottish Enlightenment," in Richard B. Sher and Jeffrey Smitten, eds., *Scotland and America in the Age of the Enlightenment* (Princeton, 1990), 228.

[21] Carl Bridenbaugh, *Early Americans* (New York, 1981), 153; Tolles, *Meeting House and Counting House*, 116–17.

[22] Tolles, *Meeting House and Counting House*, 247; Bridenbaugh, *Early Americans*, 151, 162–3; Lindley Murray, *Sequel to the English Reader* (New York, 1808), 313.

[23] Deborah C. Brunton, "The Transfer of Medical Education: Teaching at the Edinburgh and Philadelphia Medical Schools," in Sher and Smitten, *Scotland and America in the Age of the Enlightenment*, 242–59; the revelation that

Lindley Murray considered a medical career is in an unsigned, handwritten, three-page biographical manuscript at the Library of Friends' House, London, probably written by Elizabeth Frank.

[24] *Memoirs*, 19–20.

[25] Tolles, *Meeting House and Counting House*, 151–52.

[26] Norman Hampson, *The Enlightenment: An Evaluation of Its Assumptions, Attitudes and Values* (London, 1982), 288; Henry F. May, *The Enlightenment in America* (New York, 1978), 105.

[27] Francis de Voltaire, *Letters Concerning the English Nation* (London, 1733), 1–34; Peter Gay, *The Enlightenment: An Interpretation* (New York, 1977), 1: 387–88. William Tryon, colonial governor of New York and undoubtedly a friend of the Murrays, owned the entire run of the *Encyclopédie*, according to William Smith in his *Historical Memoirs: 1778-1783*, ed. William H. W. Sabine (New York, 1971), 244 (3/22/1780); see also 205–8 (1/1/1780).

[28] Lindley Murray, *Lecteur François* (Londres, 1802), 375–6, 379, 383, 389, 391, 393.

[29] Murray, *Lecteur François*, 81–90; Lindley Murray, *Introduction au Lecteur François* (New York, 1807), 52–53.

[30] *Memoirs*, 24–25.

[31] LM to JM, Sept. 5, 1803, Lindley Murray Papers, FHLS.

[32] LM to Alice Colden Willett, Feb. 6, 1805, Lindley Murray Papers, FHLS.

[33] May, *Enlightenment in America*, xvi.

[34] *Memoirs*, 27–28.

Chapter 5. The Road to Revolution

[1] Harrington, *New York Merchant*, 355.

[2] Joshua Delaplaine Papers, NYHS, Miscellaneous Microfilm, Reel 26.

[3] Thomas Jefferson Wertenbaker, *Father Knickerbocker Rebels: New York City During the Revolution* (New York, 1948), 6; John Watts, quoted in Harrington, *New York Merchant*, 42.

[4] Philip Ranlet, *The New York Loyalists* (Knoxville, Tenn., 1986), 10–25.

[5] Jackson, *Encyclopedia of New York City*, 161.

[6] Lindly, *Lindley–Lindsey–Linsley Families*, 319; Robert sold the land in 1769, once he had reestablished his fortune.

[7] *Memoirs*, 39.

[8] Alice Colden Wadsworth, "Sketch of the Colden and Murray Families," Ford Collection, NYPL, 35.

[9] *Memoirs*, 35; Flushing Monthly Meeting—New York, Certificates of Marriage 1694-1784, II, 132; FHLS (Loc. MSS 07, Acc. # 1688); see also William

Wade Hinshaw, *Encyclopedia of American Quaker Genealogy* (Ann Arbor, 1940), 3: 102.

[10] *Memoirs*, 160.

[11] *Memoirs*, 39–40.

[12] Stevens, *Colonial Records of the New York Chamber of Commerce*, 3.

[13] Stevens, *Colonial Records of the New York Chamber of Commerce*, 48 (entry for Sept. 1, 1772).

[14] NYMFS Minutes (vol. 1, 1758–1796), 11.

[15] Austin B. Keep, *The Library in Colonial New York* (New York, 1909), 114–15, 169.

[16] Barbour and Frost, *The Quakers*, 140.

[17] NYMFS Minutes, 1: 1, 11.

[18] NYMFS Minutes, 1: 15; see also Hugh Barbour et al., eds., *Quaker Crosscurrents: Three Hundred Years of Friends in the New York Yearly Meetings* (Syracuse, N.Y., 1995), 51.

[19] NYMFS Minutes, 1: 40.

[20] Merrill Jensen, ed., *English Historical Documents: American Colonial Documents to 1776* (New York, 1955), 9: 815.

[21] Robert Jay Christen, "King Sears: Politician and Patriot in a Decade of Revolution" (Ph.D. diss., Columbia University, 1968), 302.

[22] Alexander McDougall to Thaddeus Burr, Feb. 26, 1775, McDougall Papers, NYHS.

[23] Deposition of John Murray, dated March 15 and published in the *New-York Journal; or General Advertiser*, published by John Holt, March 23, 1775; unless otherwise noted, all information about the *Beulah* affair comes from this deposition; for the Joseph Reed family link, see Wadsworth, "Sketch of the Colden and Murray Families," NYPL, 27–28.

[24] The George Washington quote is from Roger J. Champagne, *Alexander McDougall and the American Revolution* (Schenectady, N.Y., 1975), 215; McDougall, a New York merchant and later a Continental Army general, came to national prominence in 1770 when he was jailed as the author of a provocative pamphlet; patriots likened his case to that of John Wilkes, incarcerated in Britain for publishing issue No. 45 of the *North Briton*; so, on February 14, 1770, the 45th day of the year, he was visited in jail by 45 friends; they dined on 45 pounds of steak cut from a 45-month-old bullock; afterwards, 45 "virgins" serenaded McDougall with 45 songs; one waggish friend asked McDougall whether his pleasure was diminished by the fact that the virgins were each 45 years old; Michael Kammen, *Colonial New York* (New York, 1975), 361–2.

[25] McDougall Papers, NYHS.

[26] Quoted in Christen, "King Sears," 302.

[27] *New York Journal*, March 23, 1775.

[28] Smith, *Historical Memoirs*, 1: 214.

[29] "Copy of a Letter which was sent by a Lady of this City, to Captain S---s, and Capt. M'D---l," March 20, 1775, Broadsides, NYHS.

[30] McDougall Papers, NYHS.

[31] Quoted in Christen, "King Sears," 303 n. 1.

[32] Arthur J. Mekeel, *The Relation of the Quakers to the American Revolution* (Washington, D.C., 1979), 102–3.

[33] "The New York Committee of Sixty to the New Haven Committee," April 17, 1775, in Morris, *John Jay: The Making of a Revolutionary.*

[34] Quoted in Champagne, *Alexander McDougall*, 78.

[35] *Memoirs*, 43–48

[36] Ranlet, *New York Loyalists*, 191–2.

[37] See, for example, William Allen Benton, *Whig-Loyalism: An Aspect of Political Ideology in the American Revolutionary Era* (Rutherford, N.J., 1969).

[38] *Memoirs*, 43.

[39] Hoff Letter Book, Park MSS. 1111, Morristown, N.J., National Historic Park Library; see also Joseph Hoff letter of June 10, 1775.

[40] Thomas M. Doerflinger, "Hibernia Furnace During the Revolution," *New Jersey History* 90 (1972): 97–114; William S. Bayley, *Iron Mines and Mining in New Jersey* (Trenton, N.J., 1910), 115.

[41] Edmund D. Halsey, *History of Morris County* (New York, 1882), 49–50.

[42] Bayley, *Iron Mines and Mining*, 115, 197.

[43] Harrington, *New York Merchant*, 46.

[44] Harrington, *New York Merchant*, 89–90.

[45] Bining, *Pennsylvania Iron Manufacture*, 140.

[46] Hoff Letter Book, June 15, 1775, and passim; Doerflinger, "Hibernia Furnace," 101.

[47] Hoff Letter Book, June 30, 1775.

[48] Gallagher, *Battle of Brooklyn*, 22–23.

[49] LM to JM, Feb. 20, 1793, FHLS.

[50] I am grateful to James Green of the Library Company of Philadelphia for searching out the *Pennsylvania Evening Post* references.

[51] Hoff Letter Book, Hoff to John Murray (Sr.), Sept. 28, 1775.

[52] Harrington, *New York Merchant*, 45.

[53] Hoff Letter Book.

Chapter 6. The Revolution and Its Aftermath

[1] William S. Baker, "Itinerary of General Washington from June 15, 1775 to December 23, 1783," *Pennsylvania Magazine of History and Biography* 14 (1890): 111–42.

[2] For one account, see "Old New York," *Evening Post,* Dec. 10, 1873, reprinted in Wilson, *Bowne Family of Flushing.*

[3] Frederick Nolan, *Lorenz Hart: A Poet on Broadway* (New York, 1994), 59, 70; Walter J. Meserve, *Robert E. Sherwood: Reluctant Moralist* (New York, 1970), 210.

[4] Gallagher, *Battle of Brooklyn,* 161.

[5] James Thacher, *Military Journal of the American Revolution* (1862; rpt. New York, 1969), 58–9.

[6] Milam Myrl Ewing, *Jacob Marion Lindley, His Ancestors and Descendants: A Genealogy* (Tulsa, Okla., 1978), 9–10.

[7] Egle, *Pennsylvania Genealogies,* 527, 533; Gallagher, *Battle of Brooklyn,* 137.

[8] *Scribner's Monthly,* February 1876, 465–6.

[9] Harry B. Weiss and Grace M. Weiss, *The Revolutionary Saltworks of the New Jersey Coast* (Trenton, N.J., 1959), 12.

[10] *Memoirs,* 45–46; Weiss and Weiss, *Revolutionary Saltworks,* 13.

[11] Weiss and Weiss, *Revolutionary Saltworks,* 12–13; a receipt for the Murrays' £200 is in the Lindley Murray papers at the NYHS.

[12] Weiss and Weiss, *Revolutionary Saltworks,* 13; *Memoirs,* 46.

[13] *Memoirs,* 48.

[14] *Memoirs,* 44.

[15] Henry Onderdonk, Jr., *Revolutionary Incidents of Suffolk and Kings Counties* (1848; rpt. Port Washington, N.Y., 1970), 24, 27, 43, 74, 75, 85.

[16] *Public Papers of George Clinton* (Albany, N.Y., 1900), 4: 511.

[17] Onderdonk, *Revolutionary Incidents of Suffolk and Kings Counties,* 43, 74–8, 85–7; Ranlet, *New York Loyalists,* 79–80, 200 n. 38.

[18] Continental Army chaplain Timothy Dwight, quoted in Herbert B. Howe, "Samuel Wood, Loyalist," *Quarterly Bulletin of the Westchester Historical Society* 23 (1947): 13.

[19] Stevens, *Colonial Records of the New York Chamber of Commerce,* 267–80, 367 n. 209; Barck, *New York City During the War for Independence,* 125–6, 238.

[20] Sabine, *Biographical Sketches of Loyalists of the American Revolution,* 2: 112–15, 560.

[21] Jackson, *Encyclopedia of New York City*, 33; Wertenbaker, *Father Knicker-bocker Rebels: New York City During the Revolution,* 120.

[22] Jackson, *Encyclopedia of New York City*, 33; E. Wilder Spaulding, *New York in the Critical Period 1783–1789* (New York, 1932), 115–16.

[23] There were Murray advertisements in nearly every issue of the *New York Packet* throughout 1784.

[24] Allott, *Lindley Murray,* 34 n. 4; s.v. Robert Murray, *Dictionary of American Biography*; *Scribner's Monthly*, February 1876, 465–6.

[25] According to an item in Stokes, *Iconography of Manhattan Island*, 6: 109, Lindley Murray actually bought the Bellevue property from Peter Keteltas (or his estate) in 1786, only after his departure from the city for England; this must been a final payment for the property, clearing the title, because it was sold on March 25, 1786; it is interesting to note that the mother of Mayor James Duane, later apparently influential in the arrangement to safeguard the Murrays' property after the Revolution, had been a Keteltas; see Leo Hershkowitz, "Federal New York: Mayors of the Nation's First Capital," in Stephen L. Schechter and Wendell Tripp, eds., *World of the Founders: New York Communities in the Federal Period* (Albany, N.Y., 1990), 30.

[26] Samuel Bowne's will, Box 6, v. 3, p. 3, Bowne Family Papers, NYPL.

[27] Champagne, *Alexander McDougall*, 203.

[28] *Independent Journal*, Dec. 29, 1783.

[29] Spaulding, *New York in the Critical Period*, 125–6; Alexander C. Flick, *Loyalism in New York During the American Revolution* (1901; rpt. New York, 1969), 72–75.

[30] Spaulding, *New York in the Critical Period,* 124.

[31] Loc. MSS. 07, Acc. #1688, p. 196, FHLS.

[32] Nancy Reid Gibbs, *Children of Light* (New York, 1986), 17.

[33] *Memoirs*, 50–58.

[34] S.v. Jacob Van Vleeck, *Dictionary of American Biography*.

[35] *Memoirs*, 55.

[36] LM to JM, Sept. 20, 1815, Lindley Murray Papers, FHLS.

[37] Champagne, *Alexander McDougall*, 211.

[38] *Memoirs*, 64.

[39] Jacob Lindley to JM, Nov. 24, 1810, FHLS.

[40] See numerous references to the departure of the *Betsy* in the *New York Packet* during November 1784.

[41] *Memoirs*, 65.

[42] Spaulding, *New York in the Critical Period*, 12, 70–72; Flick, *Loyalism in New York*, 72–75; Claude Halstead Van Tyne, *Loyalists in the American Revolution* (New York, 1902), 275–78.

[43] Champagne, *Alexander McDougall*, 211.

[44] Ewing, *Jacob Marion Lindley*, 10.

[45] Henry Adams, *History of the United States During the Administrations of Thomas Jefferson* (New York, 1986), 957.

[46] All three letters are in the Lindley Murray Papers, FHLS.

[47] Stevens, *Colonial Records of the New York Chamber of Commerce*, passim.

[48] Edmund A. Stanley, Jr., *Of Men and Dreams: The Story of the People of Bowne & Co.* (New York, 1975), 10.

[49] *Minutes of the Common Council of the City of New York: 1784–1831*, Vol. 1, *February 10, 1784, to April 2, 1793* (New York, 1917), 39–40, May 26, 1784.

[50] Henry W. Domett, *A History of the Bank of New York 1784–1884* (New York, 1884), 136–39; par value of the original shares was $500, one-third in cash and two-thirds by mortgage or deed of trust; Murray & Sansom bought six shares, John Murray one share. Robert Bowne, a Murray relative by marriage, was a director from 1784 to 1792, John Murray a director from 1789 to 1793; in a letter of February 20, 1793, Lindley instructs John Murray, Jr., to make sure all monies invested in the Bank of New York are "*in my Name.*"

[51] LM to James Duane, Lindley Murray Papers, NYHS; for numerous instances of James Duane's political astuteness, see Edward P. Alexander, *A Revolutionary Conservative: James Duane of New York* (New York, 1938) and Herskowitz, "Federal New York," 24–55.

[52] LM to Robert Murray, March 3, 1785, FHLS; *Memoirs*, 78.

[53] May, *Enlightenment in America*, 90–91.

[54] *Memoirs*, 67.

[55] Wilson, *Bowne Family of Flushing*, 101.

[56] *Memoirs*, 66.

[57] *Memoirs*, 62–63, 68–70.

[58] For example, LM to JM, Sept. 31 [sic], 1795, FHLS; it is one of many letters in which he complains of the effects of the Yorkshire climate.

[59] The will is reprinted in Lindly, *Lindley–Lindsey–Linsley Families*, 337–42.

Chapter 7. Lindley Murray's *English Reader*

[1] Malcolm Thomas in foreword to Allott, *Lindley Murray*, ix.

[2] Lindley Murray, *The Power of Religion on the Mind, in Retirement, Affliction and at the Approach of Death* (New York, 1838); *Memoirs*, 84–87; Joseph Smith, *A Descriptive Catalogue of Friends' Books* (London, 1867), 192–94.

[3] Letters of LM to JM, FHLS.

[4] Charles L. Cherry, *A Quiet Haven: Quakers, Moral Treatment, and Asylum Reform* (Rutherford, N.J., 1994), 94.

[5] Allott, *Lindley Murray*, xiii.

[6] Lindley Murray has always been known chiefly for his grammars, perhaps because they sold more widely in Britain than did his reading texts—this fame gained him the sobriquet "the Quaker Grammarian." The publication of Ingrid Tieken-Boon van Ostade, ed., *Two Hundred Years of Lindley Murray* (Münster, Germany: Nodus Publikationen, 1996), devoted mainly to studies by leading British, European and Japanese scholars of various aspects of the *English Grammar*, has, I feel, relieved me of the burden of extensive treatment of Murray's grammars; for a list of all Murray textbooks and their initial dates of publication, see "British Totals" in the Appendix to this volume.

[7] John Nietz, *Old Textbooks* (Pittsburgh, 1961), 67; Allott, *Lindley Murray*, 49.

[8] James Gilreath, ed., *Federal Copyright Records: 1790–1800*, comp. by Elizabeth Carter White (Washington, 1987), 110.

[9] Clifford K. Shipton and James E. Mooney, eds., *National Index of American Imprints Through 1800: The Short-Title Evans* (Worcester, Mass., 1969), 1: 547.

[10] Monaghan, *Common Heritage*, 55.

[11] Joshua Sharp, *Johnson & Warner's Kentucky Almanac... 1810* (Lexington, Ky., 1809), back cover; I am grateful to Jeffrey A. Douglas of the Seymour Library of Knox College, Galesburg, Illinois, for this reference.

[12] Monaghan, *Common Heritage*, 227–29, 233 n. 1.

[13] Lyman Cobb, *Cobb's New North American Reader, or Fifth Reading Book* (New York, 1844), v–vi.

[14] Ruth Miller Elson, *Guardians of Tradition: American Schoolbooks of the Nineteenth Century* (Lincoln, Neb., 1964), 6.

[15] Elson, *Guardians of Tradition*, 6.

[16] Two of the chief contributors of poetry were James Thomson and Mark Akenside, both identified with the republican tradition; see Caroline Robbins, *The Eighteenth Century Commonwealthmen: Studies in the Transmission, Development and Circumstance of English Liberal Thought from the Restoration of Charles II until the War with the Thirteen Colonies* (Cambridge, Mass., 1959), 258.

[17] The prose selections cited in the *English Reader* that have civic humanist-republican themes are: Chapter II, Sections 1, 2, 3, 5; Chapter III, Sections 1, 4, 9, 11, 12; Chapter IV, Section 5; Chapter V, Sections 12, 13; Chapter VI, Sections 1, 2, 4; Chapter VII, Section 2; Chapter IX, Sections 1, 2, 3, 4; Chapter X, Sections 12, 14, 23, 24, 25.

[18] Lindley Murray, *English Reader* (London, 1799), 153–57; these excerpts from Cicero and Sallust are among many from Roman writers in the *English Reader*, the *Introduction* and the *Sequel*. As Gordon S. Wood notes, by the eighteenth century British culture was "thoroughly infused" with admiration for "classical virtues and to that extent at least was republicanized": *The*

Radicalism of the American Revolution (New York, 1992), 101.

[19] Murray, *English Reader*, 33–37, 180–81.

[20] Ian Michael, *The Teaching of English: From the Sixteenth Century to 1870* (Cambridge, England, 1987), 196–97.

[21] See Robbins, *Eighteenth Century Commonwealthmen*.

[22] Hume gave the back of his hand to the Commonwealth Whigs in his *History of England*, but Robbins includes him with the Commonwealthmen (and I agree with her) because "he insisted that government may be changed as the good of society demands" and because of "his skepticism about royal prerogatives"; *Commonwealthmen*, 217.

[23] Blair's biographer is Robert Morell Schmitz, *Hugh Blair* (New York, 1948).

[24] Douglas Sloan, *The Scottish Enlightenment and the American College Ideal* (New York, 1971), 12–13; William Law Mathieson, *The Awakening of Scotland* (Glasgow, 1910), 213.

[25] Quoted in Jeffrey R. Smitten, "Robertson's Unfinished History of British America," in Sher and Smitten, *Scotland and America in the Age of the Enlightenment*, 165.

[26] *Ibid.*

[27] David Daiches, "The Scottish Enlightenment," in David Daiches, Peter Jones and Jean Jones, eds., *A Hotbed of Genius: The Scottish Enlightenment 1730–1790* (Edinburgh, 1986), 13.

[28] Thomas P. Miller, "Witherspoon, Blair and Civic Humanism," in Sher and Smitten, *Scotland and America*, 105–6, 108; Blair's *Lectures on Rhetoric and Belles Lettres* was widely read in America, but chiefly in a condensed version, *An Abridgement of Lectures on Rhetorick*.

[29] Blair's letter is reproduced by Elizabeth Frank in the *Memoirs*, 265–67.

[30] Quoted in Garry Wills, *Inventing America* (Garden City, N.Y., 1978), 197; it is worth noting that Blair wrote a long article on Hutcheson for the *Edinburgh Review;* see Schmitz, *Hugh Blair*, 27.

[31] "On the Slavery of the Negroes," *Introduction to the English Reader* (New York, 1809), 83 (Dialogues, Chapter 5, Section III); there are also other selections on virtuous Negroes and against slavery in the *Introduction*.

[32] William H. Herndon and Jesse W. Weik, *Abraham Lincoln: The True Story of a Great Life* (New York, 1892), 1: 34; this important fact was first noted in a discussion of Lindley Murray by Michael Belok, *Forming the American Minds: Early School-Books and Their Compilers* (Moti Katra, India, 1973), 189; the Belok book also contains an excellent essay on Lindley Murray.

[33] The connection between the *English Reader* and anti-slavery was first suggested by Michael Kraus: "Slavery Reform in the Eighteenth Century" in *Pennsylvania Magazine of History and Biography* 60 (January 1936), 65; and later in *The Atlantic Civilization: Eighteenth Century Origins* (New York, 1961).

Chapter 8. Other Murrays, Other Stories

[1] *Minutes of the Common Council of the City of New York: 1784–1831,* 1: 30.

[2] *Minutes of the Common Council,* 135.

[3] *Minutes of the Common Council,* 208.

[4] LM to JM, Sept. 30, 1815, Lindley Murray Papers, FHLS.

[5] Noah Webster, ed., *The New York Directory for 1786,* facsimile reprint (New York, 1886), 160 (July 31); the day-by-day Webster directory chose representative news items and advertisements from various newspapers.

[6] LM to JM, April 30, 1792, FHLS.

[7] LM to JM, Sept. 31 [sic], 1795, FHLS.

[8] Domett, *A History of the Bank of New York 1784–1884,* 136.

[9] LM to JM, May 2, 1808, FHLS.

[10] Domett, *History of the Bank of New York,* 139.

[11] Scoville, *Old Merchants of New York City,* 293–94; "to be a bank director," says the author of *Old Merchants,* "made any man a most important citizen and influential man; and when John Murray was made a director of the old United States Branch Bank in this city, he was a made man."

[12] Nan A. Rothschild, *New York City Neighborhoods: The 18th Century* (San Diego, 1990), 43; see also W. Harrison Bayles, *Old Taverns of New York* (New York, 1915).

[13] Scoville, *Old Merchants,* 300.

[14] LM to JM, Feb. 2, 1806, regarding disposal of brewery; also LM to JM, Nov. 2, 1807, for mention of Cunningham; FHLS.

[15] Scoville, *Old Merchants,* 301.

[16] *Memoirs,* 77.

[17] "Old New York," *Evening Post,* December 10, 1873, reprinted in Wilson, *Bowne Family of Flushing,* 102–4.

[18] Wadsworth, "Sketch of the Colden and Murray Families," 3.

[19] LM to Susannah Willett, Sept. 1, 1805, plus explanatory note attached from a Willett descendant, likely Alice Colden Wadsworth: Lindley Murray Papers, NYPL.

[20] LM to JM, Sept. 29, 1806 (replying to JM's of July 27); in the letter, before William's death, Lindley says he intends to send a set of pocket surgical instruments to William; FHLS.

[21] *Memoirs,* 106–12; Allott, in *Lindley Murray,* confused by the family name, incorrectly identifies the subject of this passage as Mary Willett: 38, n. 47.

[22] Wilson, *Bowne Family,* 101–3; Ranlet, *New York Loyalists,* 191–92.

[23] Wilson, *Bowne Family,* 101–3.

[24] Wadsworth, "Sketch of the Colden and Murray Families," 34.

[25] Wilson, *Bowne Family,* 100–3.

[26] Wilson, *Bowne Family*, 103.

[27] See LM to JM, Aug. 20, 1809; also LM to JM, Aug. 28, 1818; FHLS.

[28] JM to Catherine Murray, FHLS; see several references to the Murrays, including this trip, in Rachel Labouchere, *Deborah Darby of Coalbrookdale 1754–1810* (York, England, 1993); John's reference to "Rebukah" was obviously a joke and not just an alternative spelling; in letter 33 to James Bringhurst (FHLS), he uses the contemporary spelling "Rebeckah"; also see passing reference to the trip in LM to JM, Feb. 3, 1794, FHLS.

[29] Howard A. Kelly and Walter L. Burrage, *American Medical Biographies* (Baltimore, 1920), 907.

[30] Stewart H. Holbrook, *The Golden Age of Quackery* (New York, 1959), 34–36; see also George A. Perkins, *The Family of John Perkins of Ipswich* (Salem, Mass., 1889), 31, 59, 153.

[31] Kelly and Burrage, *American Medical Biographies*, 907.

[32] LM to JM, Dec. 30, 1805, FHLS.

[33] LM to JM, June 1, 1801, FHLS.

[34] *Memoirs*, 1, 97.

[35] *Memoirs*, ix, x.

[36] For example, LM to JM, April 4, 1806; Nov. 2, 1807; May 2, 1808; Oct. 3, 1808; Aug. 20, 1809; Oct. 30, 1809, FHLS.

[37] Perkins, *Family of John Perkins of Ipswich*, 59.

[38] LM acknowledges two letters from JM involving Rockaway; the first was started in Rockaway on August 6, 1813, and finished on August 10 in New York, indicating that JM did not escape for the entire summer; in the second, LM to JM, July 13, 1817, LM says he expects that JM is at Rockaway (both at FHLS). Rockaway abuts the village of Hibernia, indicating the Murrays may still have had an interest in the Hibernia mine.

[39] *Memoirs*, 159.

[40] Bayles, *Old Taverns of New York*, 337.

[41] Helen M. Morgan, ed., *A Season in New York: Letters of Harriet and Maria Trumbull* (Pittsburgh, 1969).

[42] Irma B. Jaffe, *John Trumbull: Patriot–Artist of the American Revolution* (Boston, 1975), 207; Trumbull and Presbyterian John were such good friends that John undertook to be the guardian of Trumbull's bastard son, John Trumbull Ray; see Theodore Sizer, ed., *The Autobiography of Colonel John Trumbull: Patriot–Artist, 1756–1843* (New Haven, 1953), 347.

[43] Morgan, *Season in New York*, 103, 111–14.

[44] Hannah Lindley Murray and Mary Murray, *The American Toilet* (New York, 1825), 3, 6; Hannah Lindley Murray and Mary Murray, *The Toilet* (Washington, D.C., 1867), preface.

[45] Gardiner Spring, *A Pastor's Tribute to One of His Flock: The Memoirs of the Late Hannah Lindley Murray* (New York, 1847), passim; the book includes some of Hannah's verse.

[46] Alfred Bishop Mason and Mary Murdoch Mason, "The Fourteen Miles Around," in Maud Wilder Goodwin, Alice Carrington Royce and Ruth Putnam, eds., *Historic New York* (New York, 1897), 318.

Chapter 9. Lindley Murray: Finale

[1] *Memoirs*, 93.

[2] *Memoirs*, 192.

[3] *Memoirs*, 93–94.

[4] LM to JM, Nov. 5, 1804, asks for "the Union Spelling-Book by A. Picket," FHLS; see also Elizabeth Frank's addendum to *Memoirs*, 136–37.

[5] LM to JM, Dec. 1, 1800, FHLS.

[6] Harry M. Warfel, *Noah Webster: Schoolmaster to America* (1936; rpt. New York, 1966), 238–9; E. Jennifer Monaghan describes Webster at the end of the *Minerva* period as "financially embarrassed and politically disillusioned": *Common Heritage*, 67.

[7] Monaghan, *Common Heritage*, 55.

[8] Noah Webster, *A Philosophical and Practical Grammar of the English Language* (New York, 1807); see also Warfel, *Noah Webster: Schoolmaster to America*, 84.

[9] LM to JM, Dec. 2, 1815, FHLS.

[10] Allott, *Lindley Murray*, 65 n. 4, quoting *The Richardsons of Cleveland* by Mrs. Boyce; *Memoirs*, 198.

[11] LM to JM, Nov. 2, 1807, FHLS.

[12] *Memoirs*, 84, 92, 95–6.

[13] LM to John Jay, July 15, 1794, in William Jay, *Life of John Jay* (New York, 1833); *Memoirs*, 188.

[14] John Jay to LM, Aug. 22, 1794, in Jay, *Life of John Jay*.

[15] *Ibid.*

[16] *Memoirs*, 188–89.

[17] *Memoirs*, 87.

[18] Jay, *Life of John Jay*, 419.

[19] This addition is evident from a reading of the *Memoirs*. Lindley refers to Jay as a "private country gentleman" who "has lived on his estate, not far from the city of New York, for many years." Jay, however, had only retired from public life in 1799, so the phrase "for many years," which occurs early in the *Memoirs* (p. 34), would not have been appropriate in 1806 when they were composed; Elizabeth Frank testifies to LM's revision of the *Memoirs* in 1823 (p. 189).

[20] *Memoirs,* 151, 170, 196.

[21] Allott, *Lindley Murray,* 38.

[22] *Memoirs,* 172.

[23] *Memoirs,* 172–4.

[24] *Memoirs,* 176.

[25] Allott, *Lindley Murray,* 44.

[26] *Memoirs,* 184.

[27] *Memoirs,* ix, 182; Bryan A. Garner, "Reconstructing Lindley Murray's Bibliographical Legacy," *AB,* Jan. 13, 1997, 73–4.

[28] Allott, *Lindley Murray,* 44 n. 4; *Memoirs,* 183.

[29] *Memoirs,* 224–5.

[30] *Memoirs,* 269.

Appendix Lindley Murray's Publishing Numbers

[1] Monaghan, *Common Heritage,* 227–29.

[2] Emily Ellsword Ford Skeel, comp., *A Bibliography of the Writings of Noah Webster,* ed. Edwin H. Carpenter, Jr. (1958; rpt. New York, 1971), 34–126.

[3] Ralph R. Shaw and Richard Shoemaker, comps., *American Bibliography* (New York, 1958); the reason for starting "the first four decades of the 19th century" at 1801 rather than at 1800 is that 1801 is the first year of the renewal of the *American Bibliography* series under Shaw and Shoemaker: originally *American Bibliography* had been begun by Charles Evans and continued (for 1799–1800) by Clifford K. Shipton; at this writing, the *American Bibliography* volumes have reached 1844; a succession of compilers have continued this valuable bibliographical work.

[4] *Memoirs,* 262.

[5] Lindley Murray, *Sequel to the English Reader* (New York, 1808), "Notice" on the back of the title page.

[6] For sample numbers of editions of Webster's *American Selection,* see Skeel, *Bibliography,* 184, 186; of his school dictionaries, 229, 257–58. In general, for Webster's non-literacy textbooks, see Skeel, *Bibliography,* 199–206, 209–17, 220–22.

[7] Smith, *A Descriptive Catalogue of Friends' Books.*

[8] Richard L. Venezky, "A History of the American Reading Textbook," *Elementary School Journal* 87 (1987): 251–2; Venezky is a leading authority on American literacy textbooks.

Selected Bibliography

Manuscripts

Columbia University, N.Y.
  John Jay Papers

New-York Historical Society, N.Y. (NYHS)
  Lindley Murray Papers
  Alexander McDougall Papers
  Joshua Delaplaine Papers

New York Public Library (NYPL)
  Lindley Murray Papers
  Bowne Family Papers
  Alice Colden Wadsworth, *"Sketch of the Colden and Murray Families"*

Morristown, N.J., National Historic Park Library
  Hoff Letter Book

Quaker Collection, Haverford College, Haverford, PA.
  Lindley Murray Papers
  Charles Roberts Autograph Collection

Friends' Historical Library, Swarthmore College, Swarthmore, PA. (FHLS)
  Lindley Murray Papers
  Minutes, New York Meeting for Sufferings
  Flushing (L.I.) Meeting, Certificates of Marriage

Library of Friends' House, London
  Lindley Murray Papers

Newspapers

  New York Gazette (Weyman)
  New York Journal (Holt)
  New York Mercury (Gaine)
  New-York Journal; or General Advertiser (Holt)
  Independent Journal (Holt)
  New York Packet (Loudon)

Published Works

Adams, Henry. *History of the United States During the Administrations of Thomas Jefferson.* New York, 1986.

Alexander, Edward P. *A Revolutionary Conservative: James Duane of New York.* New York, 1938.

Allott, Stephen. *Lindley Murray, 1745–1826: Quaker Grammarian.* York, England, 1991.

Baker, William S. "Itinerary of General Washington from June 15, 1775 to December 23, 1783." *Pennsylvania Magazine of History and Biography* 14 (1890): 111–42.

Barbour, Hugh and J. William Frost. *The Quakers.* Westport, Conn., 1988.

Barbour, Hugh et al., eds. *Quaker Crosscurrents: Three Hundred Years of Friends in the New York Yearly Meetings.* Syracuse, N.Y., 1995.

Barck, Oscar T. *New York City During the War for Independence.* New York, 1931.

Bayles, W. Harrison. *Old Taverns of New York.* New York, 1915.

Bayley, William S. *Iron Mines and Mining in New Jersey.* Trenton, N.J., 1910.

Belok, Michael. *Forming the American Minds: Early School-books and Their Compilers 1783–1837.* Moti Katra, India, 1973.

Bender, Thomas. *New York Intellect: A History of Intellectual Life in New York City, from 1750 to the Beginnings of Our Own Time.* New York, 1987.

Benton, William Allen. *Whig-Loyalism: An Aspect of Political Ideology in the American Revolutionary Era.* Rutherford, N.J., 1969.

Beyer, George R., ed. *Guide to the Historical Markers of Pennsylvania.* Harrisburg, 1991.

Bining, Arthur Cecil. *Pennsylvania Iron Manufacture in the Eighteenth Century.* 1938; rpt., Harrisburg, 1987.

Blair, Hugh. *An Abridgement of Lectures on Rhetorick.* Exeter, N.H., 1838.

_____. *Lectures on Rhetoric and Belles Lettres.* Philadelphia, 1802.

_____. *Sermons.* 2 vols. Baltimore, 1814.

Bridenbaugh, Carl. *Cities in Revolt: Urban Life in America, 1743–1776.* 1955; rpt. New York, 1971.

_____. *Early Americans.* New York, 1981.

Brunton, Deborah C., "The Transfer of Medical Education: Teaching at the Edinburgh and Philadelphia Medical Schools." In Richard B. Sher and Jeffrey Smitten, eds., *Scotland and America in the Age of the Enlightenment.* Princeton, 1990.

Champagne, Roger J. *Alexander McDougall and the American Revolution.* Schenectady, N.Y., 1975.

Cherry, Charles L. *A Quiet Haven: Quakers, Moral Treatment, and Asylum Reform.* Rutherford, N.J., 1994.

Cobb, Lyman. *Cobb's New North American Reader, or Fifth Reading Book*. New York, 1844.

Cochran, Thomas C. "An Analytical View of Early American Business and Industry." In Joseph R. Frese, S.J., and Jacob Judd, eds., *Business Enterprise in Early New York*. Tarrytown, N.Y., 1979.

Cremin, Lawrence A. *American Education: The Colonial Experience 1607–1783*. New York, 1970.

Daiches, David, Peter Jones and Jean Jones, eds. *A Hotbed of Genius: the Scottish Enlightenment 1730–1790*. Edinburgh, 1986.

Doerflinger, Thomas M. "Hibernia Furnace During the Revolution." *New Jersey History* 90 (Summer 1972): 97–114.

Dommett, Henry W. *A History of the Bank of New York 1784–1884*. New York, 1884.

Egle, William Henry. *Pennsylvania Genealogies*. Harrisburg, Pa., 1896.

Elson, Ruth Miller. *Guardians of Tradition: American Schoolbooks of the Nineteenth Century*. Lincoln, Neb., 1964.

Ewing, Milam Myrl. *Jacob Marion Lindley, His Ancestors and Descendants: A Genealogy*. Tulsa, Okla., 1978.

Flick, Alexander C. *Loyalism in New York During the American Revolution*. 1901; rpt. New York, 1969.

Gallagher, John J. *The Battle of Brooklyn, 1776*. New York, 1995.

Garner, Bryan A. "Reconstructing Lindley Murray's Bibliographical Legacy." *AB*, Jan. 13, 1997.

Gay, Peter. *The Enlightenment: An Interpretation: Vol. 1: The Rise of Modern Paganism*. New York, 1977.

Gibbs, Nancy Reid. *Children of Light*. New York, 1986.

Gilreath, James, ed. *Federal Copyright Records: 1790–1800*, comp. Elizabeth Carter White. Washington, D.C., 1987.

Goodwin, Maud Wilder et al., eds. *Historic New York*. New York, 1897.

Halsey, Edmund D. *History of Morris County*. New York, 1882.

Hampson, Norman. *The Enlightenment: An Evaluation of Its Assumptions, Attitudes and Values*. New York, 1982.

Harrington, Virginia D. *The New York Merchant on the Eve of the Revolution*. 1935; rpt. Gloucester, Mass., 1964.

Henderson, G. D. *Chevalier Ramsay*. London, 1952.

Herndon, William H. and Jesse W. Weik. *Abraham Lincoln: The True Story of a Great Life*. 2 vols. New York, 1892.

Hershkowitz, Leo. "Federal New York: Mayors of the Nation's First Capital." In Stephen L. Schechter and Wendell Tripp, eds., *World of the Founders: New York Communities in the Federal Period*. Albany, N.Y., 1990.

Hinshaw, Wade. *Encyclopedia of Quaker Genealogy*. 3 vols. Ann Arbor, 1940.

Hook, Andrew. "Philadelphia, Edinburgh and the Scottish Enlightenment." In Richard B. Sher and Jeffrey Smitten, eds., *Scotland and America in the Age of the Enlightenment*. Princeton, N.J., 1990.

Howe, Herbert B. "Samuel Wood, Loyalist." *Quarterly Bulletin of the Westchester Historical Society* 23 (April 1947).

Jackson, Kenneth, ed. *Encyclopedia of New York City*. New Haven, 1995.

Jaffe, Irma B. *John Trumbull: Patriot-Artist of the American Revolution*. Boston, 1975.

Jay, William. *The Life of John Jay*. New York, 1833.

Jensen, Arthur L. *Maritime Commerce of Colonial Pennsylvania*. Madison, Wisc., 1967.

Jensen, Merrill, ed., *English Historical Documents: American Colonial Documents to 1776*. New York, 1955.

Kammen, Michael. *Colonial New York*. New York, 1975.

Keep, Austin B. *The Library in Colonial New York*. New York, 1909.

Kelly, Howard A. and Walter L. Burrage. *American Medical Biographies*. Baltimore, 1920.

Kieran, John. *Natural History of New York City*. Boston, 1959.

Kraus, Michael. *The Atlantic Civilization: Eighteenth Century Origins*. New York, 1961.

_____. "Slavery Reform in the Eighteenth Century." *Pennsylvania Magazine of History and Biography* 60 (January 1936).

Labouchere, Rachel. *Deborah Darby of Coalbrookdale 1754–1810*. York, England, 1993.

Lamb, Martha J. *History of the City of New York: Its Origin, Rise and Progress*. New York, 1877.

Leyburn, James G. *The Scotch–Irish: A Social History*. Chapel Hill, N.C., 1962.

Lindly, John M. *The History of the Lindley-Lindsley-Linsley Families in America*. Winfield, Iowa, 1924.

Mathieson, William Law. *The Awakening of Scotland*. Glasgow, 1910.

May, Henry F. *The Enlightenment in America*. New York, 1976.

Mekeel, Arthur J. *The Relation of the Quakers to the American Revolution*. Washington, D.C., 1979.

Meserve, Walter J. *Robert E. Sherwood: Reluctant Moralist*. New York, 1970.

Michael, Ian. *The Teaching of English: From the Sixteenth Century to 1870*. Cambridge, England, 1987.

Miller, Thomas P. "Witherspoon, Blair and Civic Humanism." In Richard B. Sher and Jeffrey Smitten, eds., *Scotland and America in the Age of the Enlightenment*. Princeton, N.J., 1990.

Minutes of the Common Council of the City of New York: 1784–1831. Vol. 1. *February 10, 1784, to April 2, 1993*. New York, 1917.

Monaghan, E. Jennifer. *A Common Heritage: Noah Webster's Blue-Back Speller.* Hamden, Conn., 1983.

Monaghan, Frank. *John Jay: Defender of Liberty.* New York, 1935.

Morgan, Helen M., ed. *A Season in New York: Letters of Harriet and Maria Trumbull.* Pittsburgh, 1969.

Morris, Richard, ed. *John Jay: Making of a Revolutionary: Unpublished Papers 1745–1780.* New York, 1975.

Murray, Hannah Lindley and Mary Murray. *The American Toilet.* New York, 1825.

_____. *The Toilet.* Washington, D.C., 1867.

Murray, Lindley. *Memoirs of the Life and Writings of Lindley Murray.* York, England, 1826.

_____. *The Power of Religion on the Mind, in Retirement, Affliction and at the Approach of Death.* New York, 1838.

_____. For a list of Lindley Murray's textbooks, with year of first publication, see "British Publishing Figures" in Appendix.

Murray, Sarah. *In the Olden Time: A Short History of the Descendants of John Murray the Good.* New York, 1894.

Myers, Albert Cook. *Immigration of the Irish Quakers Into Pennsylvania.* Swarthmore, Pa., 1902.

Nietz, John. *Old Textbooks.* Pittsburgh, 1961.

Nolan, Frederick. *Lorenz Hart: A Poet on Broadway.* New York, 1994.

Onderdonk, Henry, Jr. *Revolutionary Incidents of Suffolk and Kings Counties.* 1848; rpt., Port Washington, N.Y., 1970.

Perkins, George A. *The Family of John Perkins of Ipswich.* Salem, Mass., 1889.

Public Papers of George Clinton. Albany, N.Y., 1899–1914.

Ramsay, Andrew Michael. *The Travels of Cyrus.* London, 1752.

Ranlet, Philip. *The New York Loyalists.* Knoxville, Tenn., 1986.

Ratzer, Bernard. "Plan of New York Surveyed in 1766 and 1767" (map, unpaginated insert before p. 397). In John A. Stevens, Jr., *Colonial Records of the New York Chamber of Commerce.* New York, 1867.

Reibel, David A., ed. *Lindley Murray (1745–1826): The Educational Works.* London, 1996.

Robbins, Caroline. *The Eighteenth Century Commonwealthmen: Studies in the Transmission, Development and Circumstance of English Liberal Thought from the Restoration of Charles II until the War with the Thirteen Colonies.* Cambridge, Mass., 1959.

Rothschild, Nan A. *New York City Neighborhoods: The 18th Century.* San Diego, 1990.

Sabine, Lorenzo. *Biographical Sketches of Loyalists of the American Revolution.* 1864; rpt. Port Washington, N.Y., 1966.

Schechter, Stephen L. and Wendell Tripp, eds. *World of the Founders: New York Communities in the Federal Period.* Albany, N.Y., 1990.

Schmitz, Robert Morell. *Hugh Blair.* New York, 1948.

"Schoolbooks in the United States." *American Annals of Education and Instruction* 2 (July 1832).

Schuberth, Christopher J. *The Geology of New York City and Environs.* Garden City, N.Y., 1968.

Scoville, Joseph A. (writing as Walter Barrett). *The Old Merchants of New York City.* 2 vols. New York, 1885.

Sharp, Joshua. *Johnson & Warner's Kentucky Almanac... 1810.* Lexington, Ky., 1809.

Shaw, Ralph R. and Richard Shoemaker, comps. *American Bibliography 1801* (New York, 1958); at this writing, the *American Bibliography* volumes have reached 1844; a succession of compilers have continued the work.

Shepherd, James and Gary M. Walton. *Shipping, Maritime Trade and the Economic Development of Colonial North America.* Cambridge, England, 1972.

Shipton, Clifford K. and James E. Mooney, eds. *National Index of American Imprints Through 1800: The Short-Title Evans.* Worcester, Mass., 1969.

Sizer, Theodore, ed. *The Autobiography of Colonel John Trumbull: Patriot-Artist, 1756–1845.* New Haven, 1953.

Skeel, Emily Ellsworth Ford, comp. *A Bibliography of the Writings of Noah Webster,* ed. Edwin H. Carpenter, Jr. 1958; rpt. New York, 1971.

Sloan, Douglas. *The Scottish Enlightenment and the American College Ideal.* New York, 1971.

Smith, Joseph. *A Descriptive Catalogue of Friends' Books.* London, 1867.

Smith, William. *Historical Memoirs: 1778–1783,* ed. William H. W. Sabine. New York, 1971.

Smitten, Jeffrey R. "Robertson's Unfinished History of British America." In Richard B. Sher and Jeffrey Smitten, eds., *Scotland and America in the Age of the Enlightenment.* Princeton, N.J., 1990.

Spaulding, E. Wilder. *New York in the Critical Period 1783–1789.* New York, 1932.

Spring, Gardiner. *A Pastor's Tribute to One of the Flock: the Memoirs of the Late Hannah Lindley Murray.* New York, 1847.

Stanley, Edmund A., Jr. *Of Men and Dreams: The Story of the People of Bowne & Co.* New York, 1975.

Stevens, John A., Jr. *Colonial Records of the New York Chamber of Commerce.* New York, 1867.

Stokes, Isaac Newton Phelps. *The Iconography of Manhattan Island 1498–1909.* 6 vols. New York, 1922.

_____. *New York Past and Present: Its History and Landmarks, 1524–1939.* New York, 1939.

Thacher, James. *Military Journal of the American Revolution.* 1862; rpt., New York, 1969.

Thayer, Theodore. *Colonial and Revolutionary Morris County.* Morristown, N.J., 1975.

Tieken-Boon van Ostade, Ingrid, ed. *Two Hundred Years of Lindley Murray.* Münster, Germany, 1996.

Tolles, Frederick B. *Meeting House and Counting House: The Quaker Merchants of Colonial Philadelphia.* New York, 1948.

Tully, Alan. *William Penn's Legacy: Politics and Social Structure in Provincial Pennsylvania, 1726–1755.* Baltimore, 1977.

Van Tyne, Claude Halstead. *Loyalists in the American Revolution.* New York, 1902.

Van Vleck, Jane. *Ancestry and Descendants of Tielman Van Vleck.* New York, 1955.

Venezky, Richard L. "A History of the American Reading Textbook." *The Elementary School Journal* 87 (1987): 247–65.

Voltaire, Francis de. *Letters Concerning the English Nation.* London, 1733.

Warfel, Harry M. *Noah Webster: Schoolmaster to America.* 1936; rpt. New York, 1966.

Webster, Noah, ed. *The New York Directory for 1786.* Facsimile reprint, New York, 1886.

_____. *A Philosophical and Practical Grammar of the English Language.* New York, 1807.

Weiss, Harry B. and Grace M. Weiss. *The Revolutionary Saltworks of the New Jersey Coast.* Trenton, N.J., 1959.

Wertenbaker, Thomas Jefferson. *Father Knickerbocker Rebels: New York City During the Revolution.* New York, 1948.

White, Norval. *New York: A Physical History.* New York, 1987.

White, Sheila. *Friends in York: The Dynamics of Quaker Revival 1780–1860.* Keele, England, 1995.

Wills, Garry. *Inventing America.* Garden City, N.Y., 1978.

Wilson, Edith King, comp. *The Bowne Family of Flushing, L.I.* New York, 1948.

Wood, Gordon S. *The Radicalism of the American Revolution.* New York, 1992.

Unpublished Doctoral Dissertations

Christen, Robert Jay. "King Sears: Politician and Patriot in a Decade of Revolution." Columbia University, 1968.

Murphy, Julia Nash. "Schools and Schooling in Eighteenth Century Philadelphia." Bryn Mawr, 1970.

Index